IT'S CALLED POLYAMORY

IT'S CALLED POLYAMORY

Coming Out About Your
Nonmonogamous Relationships

Tamara Pincus
and Rebecca Hiles

THORNAPPLE
PRESS

It's Called "Polyamory"
Coming Out About Your Nonmonogamous Relationships
Copyright ©2017 by Tamara Pincus and Rebecca Hiles

Thornapple Press
300 – 722 Cormorant Street
Victoria, BC V8W 1P8 Canada
press@thornapplepress.ca

Cover and interior design by Jeff Werner
Substantive editing by Amy Haagsma
Copy-editing by Roma Ilnyckyj
Proofreading by Hazel Boydell

Library of Congress Cataloging-in-Publication Data
Names: Pincus, Tamara, author. | Hiles, Rebecca, author.
Title: It's called polyamory : coming out about your nonmonogamous
    relationships / Tamara Pincus and Rebecca Hiles.
Description: Portland, OR : Thorntree Press, [2017] | Includes
    bibliographical references.
Identifiers: LCCN 2017015132 (PRINT) | LCCN 2017027078 (EBOOK) |
    ISBN 9781944934439 (EPUB) | ISBN 9781944934446 (MOBIPOCKET) |
    ISBN 9781944934453 (PDF) | ISBN 9781944934422 (PBK.)
Subjects: LCSH: Non-monogamous relationships. | Sex.
Classification: LCC HQ980 (ebook) | LCC HQ980 .P56 2017 (print) | DDC
    306.84/23--dc23
LC record available at https://lccn.loc.gov/2017015132

10 9 8 7 6 5 4 3 2

Printed in Canada.

To Eric and Alex for convincing me
I could write a book and to my poly family
for supporting me through it. — TP

To Kev, A&T, and my Femmes for always challenging me.
And to Romulus, who always loves me
(even when I don't want him to). — RH

Contents

Foreword

The year I came out was one of the most challenging in my life.

I was a divorced, white, bisexual, cisgender woman who shared custody with my ex-husband. It was 2010 in St. Louis, Missouri, the belt buckle of the Bible Belt. My daughter was ten. I owned my own home in a quiet suburban neighborhood. I had just gotten a new job at a nonprofit organization.

I thought I had the best of both worlds. By day I was a dutiful employee with good posture and proper grammar, dressed from head to toe in layers of conservative clothes. By night I was a live nude sex blogger, anonymously documenting my polyamorous life, never putting my face or name to the blog with the motto "Be open and honest."

I was already out to my partners and daughter, but not to my family and community.

Through a technology glitch that connected my identity to my blog, my employer discovered my online musings, and it inflamed them. The top blog post at the time featured a threesome role-play scene with our girlfriend.

When they fired me, it was swift and severe. I hadn't even had a chance to take off my coat when I walked into the office before the boss summoned me, her face a mask of fury.

Alarmed, I followed her to the room, where she closed the door and turned on me, icy eyes ablaze.

April 27, 2010, was the last time I was successfully slut shamed.

"*What were you thinking?*" she hissed. "You're acting like a fourteen-year-old!"

I left the building, cheeks flushed, heart racing, completely stunned and cut loose. In an instant, I went from being a model employee to a monster.

Later, my employer emailed me:

> We simply cannot risk any possible link between our
> mission and the sort of photos and material that you
> openly share with the online public. While I know
> you are a good worker and an intelligent person, I
> hope you try to understand that our employees are
> held to a different standard. When it comes to private
> matters, such as one's sexual explorations and prefer-
> ences, our employees must keep their affairs private.

For months, I searched my soul, unable to decide whether I
wanted to legally change my name and get a job at Target or
Starbucks, or fully own my sexuality and mission and put my
name and face to my sex-positive activism.

By the fall, I had made up my mind. National Coming Out
Day was Monday, October 11, 2010, and I was going to come
out nationally, irrevocably, with no turning back.

The month leading to my coming out was full of anxiety and
planning. My teeth hurt from constantly clenching my jaw in
my sleep.

I collaborated with an adult-toy company I had been doing
reviews for, as well as the local alternative weekly newspaper.

Amidst interviews and photoshoots, I struggled financially.
I was out of work and aimless.

Before the story in the local newspaper came out, I went
to my daughter's school and informed them of the upcoming
publicity. They assured me that they would never punish a
student for a parent's behavior.

When my story was released, the shit hit the fan.

I was on the cover of the magazine, nude and draped like
Aphrodite on the half shell.

For two weeks, everyone around me freaked out.

And then, it got worse.

Parents at my daughter's school were horrified by me, so I
was kicked out of my daughter's Girl Scout troop. One of the

leaders wrote me: "I'm sure you'll understand that in light of recent events you will not be invited to participate in Girl Scout programming, and somebody else will assume the role of Cookie Captain."

I was not fit to be around cookies, much less children.

And then my daughter was expelled from the school. We were told it was because they didn't have the proper resources for her.

Rumors swirled. My social media posts were reported and censored. PayPal banned me for having adult content. Detractors claimed I had sex with animals, was an attention-seeking whore, and that my child was in danger.

My ex-husband was beyond furious and shamed.

He sued me for full custody.

I was broke, desperate, and now had to hire a lawyer and invest thousands of dollars to protect myself. And then I had to educate my lawyer on polyamory and sex-positive culture.

On the verge of losing my daughter and my house, with my reputation destroyed, I was told to move out of town—I didn't belong here.

Running out of options, I shaved my head bald as a performance art legal defense fundraiser.

I was invited to tell my story at ideacity, a Toronto-based speaker series. My topic was motherhood and sexuality. My story tanked—there were people in the crowd of seven hundred who gave my talk a resounding thumbs-down. Other people pitied me.

Unemployment insurance ran out. I was going to a food bank weekly for a grocery bag of expired canned food to eat, and cleaning houses and figure modeling for cash.

As the Winston Churchill quote goes, "If you're going through hell, keep going."

Or, from Samuel Beckett: "I can't go on. I'll go on."

Life got very dark for me. I almost lost everything. But I wasn't alone. Throughout the entire ordeal, my partner remained loving and supportive, as did my lovers and sympathetic friends.

And then, in 2011, I found a job with a company that cared more about my work abilities than my personal life.

Soon after, my ex-husband dropped the custody case, a week before it was to go to trial.

I enrolled my daughter in a school system that did not judge her and provided the resources she needed.

I co-founded a local organization called Sex Positive St. Louis with three other people.

Now, my organization has more than 2,800 members.

In 2015, I was able to quit my day job and focus full time on sex and relationship consulting.

My daughter is sixteen now, and identifies as panromantic asexual polyamorous. She is a peer counselor among her LGBTQ friends. We have an amazingly close relationship.

My family accepts me for who I am. They are proud of my accomplishments and attend my events.

Incredibly, my ex-husband and I are active co-parents and on good terms. We hold family meetings and attend school functions together.

I'm self-employed and able to travel and buy anything I want at the grocery store.

I'm hired to speak at local universities on nonmonogamy. I've been featured on several sexuality podcasts. Local therapists refer their clients to me. I host spectacular play parties and educational talks. People travel from all over the country to spend time with me and enlist my services.

I am fully integrated and respected. My relationships are thriving. People admire my courage and look to me for guidance. What used to be a detraction—a polyamorous sex goddess—is now an *attraction*.

My award-winning, creative sexuality blog is a source of *pride*. Now, I can *truly* be open and honest.

And now I *really* have the best of both worlds: a rich and beautiful life, full of comfort *and* exciting adventures.

When I'm out and about, people will approach me and ask, "Hey, are you the sex-positive lady?" And then they thank me for my courage.

But wow, what an uphill battle!

There was no book like this when I was in the process of coming out. I wish there had been! I took a leap against all odds—but you don't have to.

You have this resource, this guide to coming out, on your own terms, at your own pace. No need to cut off your hair to spite your face.

Tamara Pincus is an AASECT certified sex therapist who will show you the way.

To be sure, all our actions have consequences. The reason why people hold back is because they are afraid of change. They are afraid of rejection, of punishment.

I am here to tell you that if you forge a path into the unknown, you might face adversity, but if you keep true to yourself, if you keep going, you will get past the valley of darkness and come out on top.

We all have a choice to be honest with ourselves. It takes courage.

Courage is doing the right thing, even when we're scared.

Replace the fear with love.

Read on for talking points, different perspectives, and the tools and resources you need in order to successfully come out on your own terms as polyamorous.

Let this book be your guide, your voice of reason.

Your ticket to freedom.

— Kendra Holliday, writer and editor of *The Beautiful Kind* blog, co-founder of Sex Positive St. Louis

Introduction

Our vision for this book is to provide resources to help polyamorists prepare to come out (or not), and to help monogamous people understand their polyamorous loved ones.

To start, we talk about the personal experience of coming out to yourself, as that introspection is paramount to a polyamorous person's identity. Then we expand gradually outward to discuss the unique complexities of coming out within your circles, from your partners and families to your friends and communities. Within these chapters, we include personal stories from members of the polyamorous community to offer support and accounts of experiences that may be more personalized to a polyamorous individual's situation. Some of the names in the stories were changed for privacy and protection of our polyamorous community members. Our intent is to give enough information to those interested in understanding or explaining polyamory that they are able to answer the questions of concerned individuals during the coming-out process.

In chapter 1, we first define terms and explain various types of consensual nonmonogamy as well as some complexities that affect these definitions and some aspects of polyamorous family relationships. Then we shift our focus to the social context of consensual nonmonogamy, looking first at a brief history of consensual nonmonogamy in the United States and then focusing on the current state of nonmonogamy, including cheating and infidelity, before discussing the media's influence on the increasing awareness of polyamory. While the United States shares some similarities with other cultures that practice consensual nonmonogamy, there are significant enough differences that we focus only on polyamorous relationships in the United States, as that is our area of expertise. Following the history of consensual nonmonogamy, we discuss the status of contemporary polyamory, including reasons behind the lack of cultural understanding, infidelity, and media depictions. The chapter closes with a discussion of coming out, some of the reasons people might hesitate to come out, and some of the benefits associated with doing so.

In chapters 2 and 3, we look at what people might consider before coming out—for instance, how they might personally address issues that are unique to the polyamorous individual. Some of these complexities include visibility within communities, sexually transmitted disease (STI) risk assessment, and navigating reasons for not coming out. We also discuss coming out to partners and identifying possible reactions, and finally, some strategies for handling what happens after.

Chapters 4 through 6 discuss the unique issues of coming out to families, children, and friends. Our discussion offers strategies for the polyamorous individual to identify who in their life needs the information surrounding their relationships with others. This section of the book discusses the very real challenges that polyamorous individuals might find themselves navigating in terms of familial politics, child custody, and social obligations. We offer detailed suggestions and strategies for navigating these complex relationships in a way that benefits the polyamorous person without assuming an end to the nonmonogamous relationship.

In chapters 7 and 8, we discuss the complexities of coming out at work and school, two places that are reasonably high risk in terms of potential negative repercussions. We discuss how to manage potential risk and navigate fallout after coming out in these spaces. We also discuss the unique issues that affect polyamorous people at various levels of education, and then close with a discussion on the specific concerns of how coming out as polyamorous could affect someone who is a teacher or professor.

In chapter 9, we talk about finding and creating community, specifically the importance of community to polyamorous individuals. We also discuss how to navigate various communities as a polyamorous person, from attending monogamous events with multiple partners to asking out other polyamorous individuals. We then shift our focus to generally accepted guidelines for etiquette in polyamorous communities and offer strategies on how to cultivate and be part of an inclusive community. We close with the bigger picture of community and social activism, how to identify and own your mistakes, and the general temperature of social activism in the polyamorous community.

Chapter 10 presents our hopes for you as a polyamorous person moving forward in your coming-out journey. It is our intent with this chapter to encourage you and offer you strength in whatever stage you may be working through.

Chapter 1
WHAT DOES IT ALL MEAN?
Introducing Polyamory

If you are reading this book, chances are you're not sure that monogamy works for everyone. Maybe you identify as non-monogamous, or maybe someone has recently come out as nonmonogamous to you.

We believe that monogamy should not be expected of all people. While many people are wonderfully happy within monogamy, nonmonogamous relationship structures are a valid option for a variety of people, for a variety of reasons. We do not believe that nonmonogamy is fundamentally better than monogamy. We do not claim to be more enlightened or to have reached a higher understanding than those who are monogamous. We simply believe that nonmonogamy is a valid relationship structure, and that those who feel confined by monogamy should consider the option to explore other relationship structures.

Types of Consensual Nonmonogamy

Consensual nonmonogamy is an umbrella term for any kind of relationship among partners who consent to multiple sexual relationships, regardless of whether emotional attachments are involved. This can include polyamory, swinging, designer relationships, relationship anarchy, monogamish relationships, and many other sexual practices. It can also include *polygyny*, in which a man is allowed multiple wives but women are not allowed multiple husbands, or *polyandry*, where a woman is allowed multiple husbands but men are not allowed multiple wives. However, most mainstream consensual nonmonogamy communities extend the practice to everyone, regardless of gender.

Polyamory is a type of consensual nonmonogamy in which individuals are in or open to multiple loving, romantic, and/or sexual relationships with the knowledge and consent of everyone involved. According to Morning Glory Zell-Ravenheart, one of the founders of the modern polyamory movement, polyamory is "the practice, state or ability of having more than one sexual loving relationship at the same time, with the full knowledge and consent of all partners involved." Zell-Ravenheart is credited with coining the term in an article in *Green Egg*, the official publication of the Church of All Worlds.

Swinging describes a relationship style in which a (usually) mixed-gender couple has sex with others outside of their relationship. From clubs and parties to hotel conventions and cruises, swinging takes place in a range of public and semipublic settings. Some swing parties involve mostly *soft swinging*, in which couples engage in a limited range of sexual activities with others but have penetrative sex only with the partner they brought to the party. Others involve *hard swinging*, where couples exchange partners for a broad range of sexual activities, often including penetration.

In a *designer relationship*, the participants make a set of agreements about what they think will work in their relationship. This can include a variety of activities, such as swinging, dating outside the relationship, and forming emotional bonds with others. Often, people choose this label because it does not carry the same stigma as the labels of "swinger" or "polyamorous," or because it provides a greater level of choice. Theoretically, any style of open relationship can be designed with any agreements that the partners choose.

Relationship anarchy is a style of relating in which people reject hierarchical relationship models that put sexual relationships above other forms of relationship. Instead, relationship anarchists see each relationship as an independent entity that should be considered in its own right and not in relation to external measures of value. Relationship anarchists often dismiss conventional relationship rules and lead their lives in their own unique way. Relationship anarchy is not (usually) the same as polyamory.

In practice, this means that relationship anarchists' friendships can be as important as (or even more important than) sexual relationships and that people can construct chosen families together because they want to, not because they are obligated to do so out of legal or blood ties. Also, relationship anarchists generally do not make rules to structure their relationships. As explained by sociologists and polyamory experts Dr. Elisabeth Sheff and Megan Tesene, "In relationship anarchy, no one need give anything up or compromise in order to sustain a relationship; rather, it is better to amicably separate than to sustain an unhappy and unfulfilling relationship."

Other kinds of open relationships allow for people to have sex with others outside of their relationships with the consent of their partners, without necessarily functioning as a couple or attending parties or clubs for that purpose. Frequently, gay male communities have more room for understanding where people have emotionally fidelitous relationships while having sex outside of the relationship. These types of relationships are what relationship columnist Dan Savage describes as *monogamish.*

The use of these terms is complicated by the fact that they often have different definitions depending on who is using them. Some people who are swingers hook up with new people only at parties. Others have been in relationships with the same couples for years and years and are deep friends but still identify as swingers instead of polyamorists. Some people identify as *swoly*, which is a combination of swinging and polyamory. It's important that people feel empowered to use their own labels and be responsible for their own representation of their identity.

People who identify as polyamorous can have all different kinds of sexualities, including being asexual. In fact, asexual people often find polyamory to be an ideal relationship choice because it allows them to have emotionally intimate and possibly even romantic relationships with sexual people who are still able to get their sexual needs met in other relationships. Everyone's form of polyamory is different, even when it may seem the same. For instance, one person who identifies as polyamorous may be married and see their spouse as "primary," while someone else may practice polyamory in a way where they try to never consider one partner more important than another (nonhierarchical).

Polyamorous Relationship Structures

Polyamorous relationships take a range of forms. Some polyamorous people live together, and others maintain separate housing. Children figure prominently for some polyamorous families, and others are composed of all adults.

Size

Because relationships in the United States today take such a wide range of forms, on the surface polyamorous families look much like any other married, divorced, or blended families. In her research on polyamorous families with children, Dr.

Elisabeth Sheff found that the most common polyamorous family form among her respondents was an open couple or a pair of people who live together in a marriage or marriage-like relationship, may have children and/or blended finances, and maintain sexual/romantic relationships with others. As the number of people involved in the relationship increases, there are fewer instances of those relationships (for instance, there are fewer quads than triads) and often more turnover among partners over time. Three-adult relationships can take the form of a *triad*, in which all members are romantically involved with each other, or a *V*, in which two people share the same lover but are not lovers themselves. *Quads* are relationships composed of four adults, and *moresomes* have five or more partners.

Hierarchies

Many polyamorous relationships, especially during the initial stages of defining their boundaries, establish a hierarchy of relationships in which one or more partners are designated as "primary" and others are defined as "secondary" or possibly "tertiary." Primary partners are those who maintain personal, financial, and emotional primacy, somewhat like a spouse or a "main squeeze." Some primaries are legally married, and others are bonded by depth of intimacy and time together but not legal convention. Generally, primary partners share not only sexual and emotional intimacy, but also children, finances, and/or a home. Secondary partners are usually more like girlfriends or boyfriends than spouses, probably do not live together, and most likely do not share finances or make important decisions together. Tertiary partners are generally slightly less intimate than secondary partners and considerably less intimate than primary partners, and may be in long-distance or new relationships.

Others in polyamorous relationships reject the hierarchical model of primary/secondary/tertiary relationships. One reason long-term polyamorists are suspicious of hierarchical multiple-partner relationships is that they have experienced or witnessed a "secondary" relationship that was either stunted or unable to be contained in a secondary role. The resulting pain and drama that frequently ensues when a relationship is forced to remain secondary is legendary among long-time polyamorists, and as a result they may avoid hierarchical relationships. In some cases, these nonhierarchical polyamorists categorize their relationships as nesting (living together) and non-nesting (living separately), and sometimes they do not categorize their relationships at all but simply deal with each one on an individual basis.

Configurations

There are many variations in how polyamorous people construct, organize, and maintain their relationships. *Unicorn hunters* are generally female–male couples who are seeking a *unicorn*—a bisexual woman with no other romantic attachments who is interested in hooking up with a couple. Notoriously myopic and naive, unicorn hunters are infamous in polyamorous communities for advertising for a bisexual woman between twenty and thirty-five years old to move to the couple's isolated farm and help raise their children, clean their house, and hide in the basement when company comes over so the couple doesn't have to explain her presence. In sharp contrast, most bisexual women in the polyamorous scene already have existing relationships and are rarely eager to subsume their lives into a couple's relationship. Many couples who initially approach polyamorous dating seeking that mythical unattached bisexual woman become disillusioned when she proves to be elusive, or unwilling or unable to fit the configuration the hunters envisioned. At that point, most hunters either abandon their search or broaden it to include a much wider range of partners and relationship configurations.

Another variation on the polyamorous relationship is a male with multiple female partners who are "allowed" to have only other female partners—known among polyamorous community members as the *one-penis policy* (OPP). Sometimes the policy is explicit, with clearly stated rules that prohibit the women from having sexual contact with other men. In other cases, the policy is implicit, enforced through manufactured personal emergencies and jealous tantrums when a woman attempts to see a male lover but support when she is with a female lover. The *one-vagina policy* (OVP) does not seem to be as prevalent in the polyamorous community—there is no similar popular conception of the OVP to mirror the OPP.

Some people identify as *solo polyamorists*, people who are interested in multiple partners but do not want to have a primary or nesting partner. Solo polyamorists may appear to be single folks who are dating, or they may appear to be very partnered with several people, but they probably are not married to or cohabitating with any of them. Aggie Sez, a solo polyamory blogger, explains:

Solo polyamorous people don't have, and may not want or seek, a relationship that involves entwining their life (i.e., sharing a home or finances) with any lover or partner or strongly identifying as part of a couple (triad, family, etc.) rather than as an individual. Polyamorous people may be solo by choice or circumstance, but if by choice, typically they prioritize autonomy—even when engaged in deeply emotionally invested or otherwise committed intimate relationships.

As with designer relationships and relationship anarchy, solo polyamorists choose individually how to structure their relationships, so it is hard to generalize about them.

Some solo polyamorists have an *anchor partner* to whom the solo polyamorist returns regularly and with whom the solo polyamorist spends much of their free time. Polyamory educator Cunning Minx characterizes an anchor partner as providing "support without exclusivity and a state of connectedness without implying a sexual, live-in, or hierarchical arrangement." An anchor partner is not exactly a primary partner in that the anchor does not tell their partner what to do or expect their partner to ask permission to date others. The term "anchor partner" is also used among people who do not identify as solo polyamorous. Some solo polyamorists endorse relationship anarchy as well.

Intersectionality with Sexual Identity and Race

Sexual and cultural identities can have a great impact on the ways in which people experience life as polyamorists. For instance, in mainstream gay male culture nonmonogamy is considered a norm. In mainstream heterosexual culture, on the other hand, people are expected to remain (or at least appear to be) monogamous. Many people in consensually nonmonogamous communities covet bisexual women as partners, though bisexual men are generally not seen in the same light. Most consensually nonmonogamous community members seem to accept bi women's desire to be polyamorous because it is understood that bi women may want to have partners of more than one gender. As a result, in some ways it can be easier for bi people—and especially bisexual women—to come out as polyamorous than it is for straight people or lesbians.

Race and culture can also have an effect on the coming-out process. For a person of color, to come out as polyamorous is to take on another stigmatized identity, which can be an extra risk. The prevalence and influence of religion in African American communities often make Black polyamorous people feel less able or willing to come out for fear of judgment by their communities. There is a similarly high level of religiosity that can come into play in Latinx cultures. In some Latinx cultures it is expected that men will cheat, so if Latino men come out as polyamorous they may encounter either greater understanding because of stereotypes that Latino men are highly sexual, or greater stigma due to that perception of being highly sexual. When women come out as polyamorous, they are often judged more harshly because of religious ideas about purity and a sexual double standard.

In the United States, ideas about coming out (indeed ideas about almost everything) are shaped primarily by White people's thoughts and experiences. Current popular opinion demands that sex and gender minorities come out to gain visibility, political representation, and human rights. What these demands overlook are the experiences of people of color in their home communities, in White mainstream LGBT communities, and in society at large. When White people come out, they come out into a gay, lesbian, trans, polyamorous, or other kind of community that is almost certainly predominantly White and run by White people who will virtually always interact with them in what appears to be a racially neutral way. When people of color come out, they have deal with the same kinds of stigma from their families of origin (the family a person comes from, whether by birth, adoption, or choice) with which White people contend. On top of that, however, they also often deal with racism from other LGBTQ community members, possible accusations from family and friends that they are traitors to "real" people of color, and higher levels of negative judgment from society at large. In short, people of color have a lot more to lose and not nearly as much to gain by coming out, so White people need to give people of color space to come out in their own time and for their own reasons. It is a completely legitimate choice to remain closeted, to reach an understanding with family and friends by being vague without explicitly coming out, or to come out very selectively to carefully chosen confidants. This book should not be read as a mandate for all polyamorists to come out at every minute, but rather as a guide to a larger coming-out process that will vary significantly with each individual's social setting and life experiences.

History of Nonmonogamy in the United States

Casual dating, nonmonogamy, and hookup culture are not new. They also haven't changed much over the years; they simply have a title now.

The 1800s: Free-Love Transcendentalists

In the mid to late 1800s, several groups of people in the United States practiced a multiple-partner relationship style, most influenced by the nineteenth-century transcendentalism movement. Brook Farm was an experimental free-love community that "challenged conventional Christian doctrines of sin and human unworthiness." The Oneida Community, founded in 1848 by John Humphrey Noyes, established a system of "complex marriage" in which "each male was theoretically married to each female, and where each regarded the other as either a brother or a sister." Nashoba was a free-love community established in 1862 by Frances Wright, a wealthy Scottish immigrant who formed a large communal farm, "bringing together both free blacks and whites to work and make love." She opposed racism and declared "sexual passion the best source of human happiness."

Outside of communal or utopian groups, conventional society in the United States was hostile to nonmonogamy of any form. A primarily Christian nation, the United States judged adulterers or "libertines" who had sex outside of marriage harshly, both legally and socially. As in other cultures and eras, upper-class men had access to mistresses, and any man who could afford it had access to prostitutes, but women had far less sexual freedom. Divorce was incredibly scandalous, and some people questioned whether allowing a widowed woman to remarry was tantamount to "lawful adultery."

The 1900s: Sexual Revolution to Internet Revolution

The idea that your partner should be your best friend, your lover, and a source of community is a new one, and it did not become popular until the early 1900s, gaining momentum in the economic upswing following World War II. In the period immediately prior to this, women and men led more or less separate lives, socializing primarily with members of their own gender. Also, living situations were far more communal and multigenerational, leading to a sense of community between tenants and other family members.

The 1960s and 1970s witnessed an explosion of gay and feminist agitation for rights and the evolution of countercultural groups and sexual practices. Begun in the 1950s among military families, swinging really took off in the 1960s and 1970s, with swing clubs opening in major cities and suburbanites throwing "key parties," at which heterosexual couples would meet up, put their car keys in a bowl, pick out different keys, and then fool around or have sex with the owner of the new set of keys. In the 1960s, because of the sexual revolution, sexual activity became more liberated and casual sex more commonly accepted.

Polyamorous communes also evolved in the late 1960s and early 1970s. In Los Angeles, John and Barbara Williamson established the Sandstone Retreat. Kerista, possibly the most influential nonmonogamous, protopolyamorous intentional community, was based in the San Francisco Bay Area between 1971 and 1991. Maura Strassberg, a professor at Drake University who specializes in sexuality and the law, noted that Kerista lasted for twenty-five years with an "experimental lifestyle that included group marriage, shared parenting, total economic sharing, a group growth process, and a utopian plan for improving life around the world by replicating their model of community living."

Once the sexual revolution collided with the spread of AIDS and other STIs in the 1980s, consensual nonmonogamy lost some of its luster and went underground to a degree. The 1990s brought the advent of Internet communication, and with it the beginnings of a resurgence of interest in consensual non-monogamy. The Internet has proved an especially important site for community building among marginalized populations because it has allowed people to find each other in the privacy of their own homes. Sex and gender minorities have populated the Internet in droves, forming personal, sexual, and community connections online.

Social expectations of what marriage should be changed significantly over the twentieth century. In those short hundred years, marriage went from being a property transaction to being a relationship based on love. There has been a remarkable change in gender roles, including a departure from the assumption that women are property. With this expansion of the freedom of women, the ideal that the man is the primary breadwinner and provider for the family has also changed. As women's rights have grown and shifted to allow more access to education, employment, and reproductive options, so too has marriage changed to become less of an arrangement for security and more of a match between equal partners.

Cultural Context of Polyamory

The general public often (mistakenly) negatively attaches polyamory to one of two concepts: religion and infidelity.

Religion

Most popular information surrounding polyamory has come in the form of nonmonogamy within a religious context. Much of the public perception of abuse or coercion within polygamous relationships comes from the Fundamentalist Church of Jesus Christ of Latter-Day Saints, a branch of the Mormon religion that practice plural marriages that have resulted in arrests and allegations of abuse and incest. Linking or equating polyamory with polygamy—and therefore abuse, incest, or coercion—can create a hostile environment for polyamorous people.

In the United States, the infidelity rate is approximately 30 to 40 percent in unmarried relationships, and 18 to 20 percent in marriages. So it is understandable that people outside of polyamorous communities are confused by the concept that polyamorists can openly date outside of their "primary" relationship. Infidelity and deception create pain and harm, and most people have been or know someone who has been on the receiving end of infidelity. Some people's negative reactions to coming out can be traced to a misunderstanding of the emphasis on openness and communication in nonmonogamy that erroneously links all multiple-partner relationships with cheating, deception, and harm.

Although many people associate casual dating and hookup culture with twentysomething millennials, nonmonogamy is neither new nor uncommon. The very existence of hookup culture and casual dating implies that there is not necessarily a presumption of monogamy in one's twenties. There is, however, no evidence to say that today's twentysomethings are having any more sex than those in previous generations. In fact, studies show that the number of sexual partners people have and the frequency at which they change have not changed in recent generations. What has changed dramatically is the way sexually active adults view and report their sexual activities. This flexible attitude toward monogamy means that young people are often negotiating their relationships and safer-sex agreements. Such negotiation implies awareness and possibly even consent. Much contemporary nonmonogamy, though, is neither negotiated nor consensual.

Infidelity

Definitions of infidelity and cheating are as slippery as they are numerous, hinging on questions of time (cheating just right now or ever in the life of the relationship?) and degree of contact (from clandestine emotional chats to intercourse). In their study of the attitudes of couples counselors toward infidelity, researchers Naomi Moller and Andreas Vossler found conflicting definitions of what counted as cheating. They concluded that infidelity is socially constructed differently in different circumstances by different people.

Cheating is quite prevalent in the United States today, and even those who publicly espouse monogamy are often exposed as cheaters who don't practice what they preach. The exposure of Josh Duggar, one of the subjects of the TV show *19 Kids and Counting*, when the client list for cheating website Ashley Madison was released is just one in a very long line of famous "monogamists" who were caught cheating on their partner. More mundane people do it too, and for a variety of reasons. One study suggests that infidelity is linked to age, religious behavior, and educational level. Researchers also agree that opportunities for cheating in apparently monogamous relationships have expanded significantly with the advent of Internet communications.

One reason cheating is so common in the United States today is the lack of conversation about the definition of relationships. A primary difference between polyamory and cheating is that polyamory is done ethically and openly, with everyone's consent. Within consensual nonmonogamy communities, conversations regarding the definition of a relationship are extensive, partly because of the number of people involved, and partly because of a mutual desire to ensure that all parties are on the same page. In traditional monogamous relationships, however, most people begin with preconceived notions of what relationships are supposed to be, as well as how the parties involved are supposed to adhere to the "natural" progression of the relationship.

Notions of conventional monogamy overlook the numerous ways in which people interact with their surroundings and change over time. All too often people in monogamous relationships end up feeling betrayed if their partner behaves in a way that they do not define as monogamous; however, people routinely disagree about what monogamy is supposed to look like. An excellent example is the difference between emotional cheating, with talking but no sex, and physical cheating, which includes sex but may or may not include talking. Some monogamous partners feel no betrayal in the case of an office flirtation that remains "hands off," while others may feel absolutely crushed by the implied intimacy and personal attraction.

Media Awareness of Polyamory

The recent explosion of books, TV shows, movies, websites, and articles about polyamory leaves some people wondering why there are so many polyamorous people these days. One of the main answers is that the general public has become increasingly aware that polyamory exists and is, for some, a valid relationship option. With the avalanche of media exposure to consensual nonmonogamy, people are learning more about polyamory, and some are considering whether it is right for them. The more exposure that the media gives nonmonogamy and polyamory, the more people learn that it is a valid option for their relationships as well.

Conventional Media

Conventional media coverage has also spread the word about polyamory, in part due to a fascination with sex, and in part due to an interest in different lifestyles. Unfortunately, and predictably, the media often paints an incredibly sensation-alized image of polyamorous people. Showtime's *Polyamory: Married & Dating* covers the supposed reality of polyamory. While the show does portray some of the more complicated issues and configurations within polyamory, it does so through a highly sexualized lens. *Big Love*, another reality show about consensual nonmonogamy, focuses on a Fundamentalist Mormon family with one husband and four wives. While it does not present the more egalitarian relationship structures that are often found in polyamory, it still provides another image of consensual nonmonogamy to consider. Polyamorous email lists and websites overflow with casting calls for non-monogamous or polyamorous people for reality shows, and many request people who are secretly living nonmonogamous lifestyles or who can bring drama into their lives.

Social Media

Social media also plays a significant role in the growing aware-ness of consensual nonmonogamy. The Internet has provided subcultures of all stripes with a wonderful resource for finding people with similar viewpoints who can help create a sense of community. Polyamory's explosion has spread with social media to include extremely popular pages on Facebook and reddit, personal stories of polyamorous individuals on blogs such as *Poly Role Models* and *the Open Photo Project*, thriving discussion spaces like the *r/Polyamory* board and the Loving More website, and groups like the Polyamory Leadership Network and PolyResearchers discussing political and aca-demic issues relevant to polyamory. Consensual nonmonog-amy is also a common topic of discussion on the kink social media site FetLife. All of this adds up to hundreds of thousands of polyamorous people talking openly about their lives online, and those numbers keep getting bigger every day.

If you start talking about polyamory on Twitter or Facebook, people will eventually figure out that you are probably polyamorous yourself, or at least an ally of polyamory. This awareness can make things both easier and harder. It can allow you to skip the "I'm polyamorous" conversation because people will already know, but some people may stop talking to you without having any conversation as to why. Often when you're speaking about polyamory on social networks, people view you as a person who is living the life they want but are afraid to get. You may become a resource for them, an example of how to live the life they want. If you are comfortable with it, you can become what sex educator Kate McCombs calls a "beacon of permission"—a person who empowers others to make choices because they know someone who is polyamorous. This can lead to a domino effect or, as Rebecca likes to call it, a "polynation," wherein you're pollinating people with your ideas, which they take and bloom into something beautiful.

Sensationalized Sexualized Expectations

While media exposure can provide an excellent introduction to polyamory, it can also lead to some unrealistic expectations. Many people who consider embarking on a polyamorous relationship erroneously assume that polyamory is all sex all the time and that it doesn't include much relationship processing or commitment. Others may feel that they are supposed to behave in a certain way or adopt a certain structure when opening their relationship. For instance, they may feel that the only way to start out as polyamorous would be to have a triad or a quad, as opposed to a V or a more open relationship style. Skewed media portrayals emphasizing sex over communication and the unrealistic expectations they produce too often amount to trouble for the newly polyamorous relationship and possibly an increased chance of negative outcomes.

One way sensationalized media stories contribute to misinformation about polyamory is by presenting it as a way to come back from infidelity. The scenario usually involves a relationship where one partner cheats and then attempts to coerce their initial partner into accepting this relationship structure into their lives. Another popular sensationalizing tactic is to emphasize the sexual component of polyamory. There is nothing wrong with people who are polyamorous and also enjoy sex (casual or otherwise), but implying that polyamory is simply a way for people in committed relationships to cheat on their partners by having wild sexual encounters is simply not true. In addition, the focus on polygynous families emphasizes a version of consensual nonmonogamy that is not equitable to women who would want partners of the opposite sex. And because the mainstream camera gaze prefers to focus on White, conventionally attractive, middle-class people doing risqué things, they tend to be the center of the polyamory shows. This small slice of people then becomes the basis for assumptions about the way all polyamorous people live, raise children, and interact with others. Until more people feel safe being open about their lifestyles, media portraits will have a hard time being representative of most polyamorous people.

Chapter 2

WHAT TO CONSIDER WHEN COMING OUT

As media attention and public awareness of polyamory increase, more and more people are beginning to come out as polyamorous. While this can be tremendously exciting and provide immense relief for the people who come out and feel more comfortable in a polyamorous lifestyle, it is likely to raise a number of questions from friends and families. The coming-out process can go far more smoothly when polyamorists are equipped with information that can help their friends and family understand and relate to consensual nonmonogamy.

In this section, we discuss reasons that can make people hesitate to come out, including vulnerabilities that are specific to polyamorists, concerns about intrusive questions from others who are curious about polyamorous relationships, and finally some of the benefits that can result from coming out. We also respect the choice of people to *not* come out—it makes the most sense in a lot of situations.

Vulnerabilities of Polyamory

People might stay "in the closet" about their polyamory for many reasons, including a lack of safe spaces, a lack of anyone safe to talk to, and a lack of understanding. Most of the reasons for staying in the closet are based in fear. Whether it's fear of losing a job, housing, children, family, or friends and community, the outcome is the same. People keep a part of themselves hidden to protect something they care about: themselves.

Much of the trouble with coming out as polyamorous comes from the specific vulnerabilities that surround polyamorous people. Many things can feed the fear of coming out, but the most important is a lack of information on coming out. Currently, there are few resources for the person coming out to fall back on to feel safe about their decision. It is likely that there will be more resources available as polyamory is legitimized and supported in our culture.

Visibility

Contemporary culture in the United States has not shifted to identify more than two people as legitimately being in a romantic or sexual relationship. When two people are together and look intimate, onlookers are likely to assume that those two people are together in a romantic relationship. When three people are together and any combination of the three appears to be intimate together, an outsider might only identify two as being partners. When someone is in a relationship with more than one person, they can sometimes feel anxious or isolated when an outsider does not validate the existence of their relationship. That anxiety and feeling of isolation can foster worries that they or their relationship is "less than" other relationships that are seen or treated as valid. Unfortunately, remaining closeted can amplify feelings of anxiety and isolation and contribute to a cycle of hiding, invalidation, invisibility, and further isolation.

Sexually Transmitted Infections

If media discussion is any gauge, many people outside of the polyamorous community believe that polyamorous people engage in promiscuous sexual practices that put them at risk of contracting and spreading sexually transmitted infections (STIs). Depending on what kinds of sex you are having with what kinds of partners, having multiple partners can increase your risk for STIs. Ironically, though, research shows that people in polyamorous and other consensually nonmonogamous relationships are less likely to transmit or contract an STI. Studies find that much of STI transference in ostensibly monogamous relationships is linked with a lack of STI protection in infidelity. Communication within the polyamorous community about such topics as STI protection preferences, number of current partners, testing frequency, and boundaries appears to help in keeping the STI rate down.

Employment and Housing

Some employers with conservative values include morality clauses in their employment contracts that allow the employers to fire an employee who violates specified moral standards. (Think Chick-fil-A or Hobby Lobby, two notable employers who have recently come under fire for their conservative views on LGBTQ rights and access to birth control.) Infractions include everything from crimes such as getting a DUI, being busted for drug possession, or embezzling money, to a range of sexual offenses that would definitely include polyamory. Thus, employers can fire people for being polyamorous.

Similarly, many cities have local zoning regulations that limit the number of unrelated adults living together. These

laws are usually drafted with the intention of limiting frater-
nities and sororities, and preventing immigrants from trying
to fit "too many" people in a house or apartment. However,
these regulations are sometimes selectively enforced against
sex and gender minorities like polyamorists when a landlord
is uncomfortable with tenants' sexual or gender identities
and expressions.

Children and Families

One of the vulnerabilities that can keep polyamorous folks
in the closet is the fear of how being out might impact their
families. Members of the public often associate sex and gender minorities with dangerous sexual "deviance" like rape or
molestation, and polyamory conjures images of wild orgies in
some people's minds. Conventional concerns include the fear
that children could be damaged emotionally, sexually, or physically by a parade of adults moving through their lives. Because
more than two of the adults in polyamorous families are sexually connected, members of the public often become distracted
with the idea that sexuality is rampant all over the household
in every setting at every moment. In such an inflamed imagination, there is no room for the real mundanity of doing dishes
and folding laundry that more typically characterizes a polyamorous family's life.

The erroneous assumption that polyamorous families
are saturated in sex makes the general public nervous about
polyamorous parenting—and when people get nervous about
parenting, custody gets called into question. For polyamorous
families, the people most likely to attempt to wrest custody of
their children away from them on the grounds that the polyamorous folks are inappropriate or unsafe parents are, first,
their own parents (the children's grandparents), second, their
ex-spouses, and, a distant third, the state or Child Protective
Services.

Even when legal custody does not become an issue, some people experience very strained relationships with their families of origin—that is, the family a person comes from, whether by birth, adoption, or choice—when they come out (or are outed by someone else) as polyamorous. Parents might reject their polyamorous children, and brothers and sisters might ostracize their polyamorous siblings. However, research from other sex and gender minorities indicates that even if the family of origin's initial reaction to their loved one's coming out is negative, sometimes family members change and grow more accepting over time.

There are no legal protections that we know of for polyamorous people. They can lose their children, jobs, and housing, and have no legal recourse to pursue remedy for discrimination. With the growing popularity and visibility of polyamory, it is likely to be only a matter of time before there is a test case that establishes rights for polyamorous parents, but until then the personal and legal vulnerability that comes with polyamory is a real concern for some polyamorous folks.

A Note About Intrusive Questions

As a polyamorous person, you are not required to tell anyone anything about your situation. Unfortunately, there's not always a graceful way to decline someone's concern. If you are uncomfortable educating them or continuing a conversation where the validity of your relationships or your competence in choosing partners or a path that makes you happy is being questioned, then a simple "Thank you for caring. I appreciate your concern; however, that's not what is happening, this is what is happening" will suffice.

Benefits of Coming Out

Most of the research on coming out as a sexual minority has been conducted with people who have come out as gay or lesbian. Results indicate that rather than being a single event that someone completes once or a unified experience that happens in the same way and with the same effect for everyone, coming out is a process that varies tremendously by who is doing it and their social settings. Depending on who you are and what is happening in your life, coming out as polyamorous can be vitally important and extremely personal, or it can be of little consequence. If you are reading this book, chances are that coming out poses some issues for you. If so, you are in good company, because there are valid reasons that it might create some friction. Benefits of coming out include improved mental health, protection of your physical health, and public recognition

Mental Health

For some polyamorous folks, especially those who identify as inherently polyamorous, attempting to live a monogamous life can be absolutely excruciating. Trying to force themselves to live in a way that does not match their internal experiences takes a tremendous toll on some polyamorists, and the price of being in the closet can be quite high when it comes to mental health and self-esteem. Coming out as polyamorous can mean relief, authenticity, and emotional intimacy.

Relief
Once they find that they identify as polyamorous, people may feel a tremendous relief from the pressures they had previously felt in monogamous relationships. Like taking off a pair of tight jeans, letting go of a monogamous identity and practice can

allow a polyamorous person to breathe deeply and see who they really are without that external and ill-fitting structure.

Authenticity and Emotional Intimacy

Coming out is also important for people who value being open and honest with the people in their lives. Keeping a secret from siblings, parents, friends, and children can be very stressful, and feeling that you cannot share your whole self with your loved ones can be sad and alienating. Being able to speak honestly about who you love and what you do in your free time allows you to be yourself with family and friends.

Physical Health

The open and honest communication that you create from coming out to your partners will help in STI risk assessment. Polyamorous community norms include not only extensive communication, but also regular testing for STIs so that people are able to assess their own status and their partners' risk. Regular testing, combined with strong communication skills, contributes to lower rates of STI transmission among consensually nonmonogamous people than among cheaters.

Public Recognition

Beyond the mental and physical benefits of coming out, the process of coming out can help others who are disillusioned with monogamy learn that there are more choices than just monogamy and cheating. This sort of visibility will eventually help to create more exposure and acceptance for polyamorous relationships and families. Unfortunately, the current lack of exposure affects the number of polyamorous people coming out, for fear that they will lose their families, jobs, or social standing in the community. Ideally, with more exposure will come more change, and the change will address the lack of employment and housing protections for polyamorous families.

The mainstream LGBQ* movement has made great strides in the past ten years in promoting same-sex marriage and employment protections. These strides are directly linked to large numbers of LGBQ people coming out and demanding recognition in the 1990s and early 2000s. Gay liberation movements have had quite a lot of success in changing the laws and attitudes toward LGBQ people and families. Already riding on the coattails of the gay liberation movement, the polyamorous community would be well served to use that model when increasing visibility to further politicize the polyamory movement.

§

What to Consider When Coming Out Stories

A Mono Guy Stretches His Envelope for the Love of a Woman
T and I had been together for about six months when she first heard the word "polyamory," and she began to identify with it instantaneously. At first I was quite taken aback and was just not sure what to think. She began dating, and I checked it out enough to get a good sense of it. About ten months into our relationship, I realized that I was pining for T to care that I was monogamous, but that it was *I* who needed to care if I was monogamous. After I sat with it and thought about it deeply for another couple of months, I decided that I was truly a monogamous person and that if T really needed polyamory then we should break up. I was fine

---

* Here we say LGBQ instead of LGBTQ because, while the transgender movement has been incredibly important to the LGBTQ movement, we feel that it does a disservice to members of the transgender community to imply that they have reached the same legal and social status as other members of the LGBQ community. We sincerely hope that attitudes and laws change in the future to be more inclusive of our Trans* family and friends.

with her wanting polyamory, but I was not sure that I could want it with her.

T decided that she would rather be with me and be monogamous than be without me and be polyamorous, so we stayed together. For five years I watched as she slowly wilted, becoming extremely restless and increasingly unhappy. She had lost interest in sex—and that is saying a lot, because she has the highest sex drive of any partner I have ever met. The sparkle was completely gone from her eyes, and I could see that monogamy was wearing on her like a lead apron. She obviously tried to make the best of it, but it was just as obviously tearing her up inside.

Gradually I began to feel more and more secure in my relationship with T and started to appreciate that she had been living the way that I had wanted to live. Over the five years that we had been together monogamously I realized that I felt very respected in my monogamy and that T had not pushed or demanded polyamory but gone along with my monogamously oriented life. As I relaxed more and more into my relationship with T, I began to realize that I could tolerate the stretch of polyamory, like a yoga pose I could not do for a long time but eventually settled into. It became very clear that I would rather be in a poly relationship that worked well than a monogamous relationship that did not.

It was the working well part that was the clincher—so many of the poly relationships I witnessed emphatically did not work well and in fact looked like a complete disaster. I did not want that, but I certainly did not want a stunted and shattered version of the woman who had once been so vibrant, either. It took a while, but I came to think that it might be less painful for me to explore polyamory than it would be for T to be monogamous.

We learned a lot in our first serious poly relationship—a quad with another couple who eventually broke it off and broke our hearts. Rebounding, we both started dating other people, and T fell madly in love with Q around the same time that I fell hard for S. S felt the same way about me, and it became clear to both of us that we would rather be monogamous with each other than in a poly relationship at all. It was painful, and T and I seriously considered breaking up, but I decided to stick it out because I simply did not want to walk away from my relationship with T unless it appeared to be absolutely unworkable. It has been messy and difficult, and we have hung on the brink of breaking up many times. Numerous times I have thought, *Holy crap! How are we going to negotiate this?*

Now T is in love with a different person and I am dating a couple of people who are dear friends. I love them, but we are not *in* love with each other the way that I was with S. I fear that if I meet another person like S and fall in love again, the same issue of wanting to be monogamous with that person will come up again. I know that I love T and that I am fundamentally intact as a person, so I am okay. But I am constantly asking myself if this is really what I want to do, and I have yet to answer. The process we are in is dynamic and is good more often than it is not, but is it the right thing for me? I truly don't know.

I used to feel victimized, like my love for T was betrayed, and my head would explode every time I thought about her having sex with someone else. I no longer feel betrayed or victimized, and I am fine with her having sex with other people. Having her fall deeply in love with someone else and want to have babies with him still makes my head explode, but we shall see what happens with that over the years. Because I have invested so much in this relationship and T is such an amazing person, I think our lives together are ultimately workable. This only works for us because we are so willing to work hard with each other to make things work, using specific relationship skills (like The Work of Byron Katie) that make it worthwhile to be together. We have had countless experiences that make it possible for us to be honest and loving with each other and move beyond our difficulties in a unique way that lets us go deeper. However, if someone at the beginning of their poly-mono relationship asked me if they should give it a try, I would say no, definitely not, just walk away. If you don't have a lot motivating you and a skillful means of applying that motivation then it is just masochistic to attempt a poly–mono relationship.

When I think about coming out myself, it boggles my mind. It is true that my wife and I both have relationships with others that are ongoing, loving, and out in the open, which sounds a lot like polyamory. But in my heart, I would rather be monogamous. Polyamory is like a second language to me: I can speak it with some challenge, but I do not dream in it and my deepest heart does not bend that way. Monogamy is my native tongue. So am I polyamorous? Am I a monogamous person having polyamorous relationships? If I were to come out, what exactly would I come out as?

I would like to say that I have grown and discovered miraculous things, and that would be true. I could also say that it has been codependent and I have been doing something that does not really fit me for years, which would also be true. At some point I thought we could try polyamory like we had tried monogamy, but that genie is out of the bottle now and never going back in. I identify as more poly and less monogamous than I did ten years ago. To be happy in a poly relationship, I have had to learn to identify what was in it for me, not just focusing on what I was missing in monogamy, but also what I could get out of polyamory. After that it got a lot easier, which is to say it is still not easy, just a bit easier!

— White, heterosexual, cisgender man

Sarah Comes Out on TV

When I was in my mid-forties, my nesting partner, his other partner, and I were preparing to be interviewed on our local TV station about polyamory. I was excited and scared; we all three lived together in a group house with other people. Up until then I hadn't really gone deeper with my metamour (my partner's partner). She wasn't big into clothes, so the three of us did some clothes shopping for the interview. We recruited one of our housemates to do a practice interview, which was a lot of fun for all of us. He asked really great questions and I learned things about my metamour that I had not known before. It was a great opportunity to go deeper. When the TV crew came, the whole interview experience was fun and exciting. The piece that actually aired represented us really well. It was scary to have it out in the public in our local community, but nothing bad came of it.

— White, bisexual, cisgender woman

Rebecca Puts One Toe Back into the Closet

When Wes and I met, I knew he was polyamorous and married. He knew I was polyamorous and in the middle of a divorce. We knew he had to move back to his home state after his job wrapped up, but on our first date, we just clicked. We were lost in new relationship energy (the surge of excitement when a relationship first starts and everything is shiny and new) and the rush of compatibility, so when Wes moved home we found ways of making our relationship work. Our relationship grew over a span of months, and it was wonderful.

Through all our compatibility and communication, I found a weak spot. I am out. I am so very out. I am out in every blog post, every Facebook status update, every tweet. Wes is not. Wes is not out to his family; he and his spouse are not out to his in-laws. He is out to a few people and regularly tells me he's out to the people who matter the most in his life. Regularly reminds me that he acknowledges that I am an important part of his life to the people who matter most to him. That acknowledgement means everything to me. That visibility in his life means everything to me.

Even still, it's hard. It's hard to be a polyamorous person who loves another person who can't—for whatever reason—be with you in certain situations. It can feel like you're a secret, or that someone's ashamed of you. It is even harder when you know there are no easy solutions. For Wes and me it was a matter of identifying where we could compromise. Social media and my blog are a huge part of my life. I don't live near my family or most of my friends, so I keep up with them through social media. Having to hide a part of my life from them was actually painful for me.

So, Wes and I came up with a solution. He took on the name Wes as an identifier in my life and my spaces. We agreed to keep his photo off Facebook, unless the photo was set to "friends only," as the site's algorithms would make it too easy for him to be outed by accident. I was free to post anything I wanted about Wes on my other social media forums. It still isn't great, and I still get frustrated that I can't post about him on Facebook, which is where my biggest network exists.

It is important for me to remember that it is an individual journey. Wes's not being out affects me, absolutely, but my being out has the potential to affect him far more. It is vital for me to be more concerned with the safety of my partner physically, emotionally, and financially than I am with my desire to share my personal life publicly. The best things about boundaries is that they may be renegotiated at a later date.

I know Wes and I will continue to keep things open. He makes space for my frustrations that I'm not visible in his life, as a response to my changing my nature to respect his boundaries. This balance, this compromise, this constant communication about what is and isn't acceptable in our relationship is what will keep it strong, even when it's hard. Coming out is a process, and everyone comes to it differently. It's important for relationships where people are at different stages of being out to focus on empathy, boundaries, compromise, and the love they have for each other.

— White, bisexual, cisgender woman

Nudism Okay, Polyamory Not Okay

I was refused membership in a nudist colony because I had two partners. Their position was "What would the odd man out be doing?" I couldn't get them to understand that both men were involved with me. My current relationship formation is my husband and two other women. He took us all out for dinner recently and the waiter was amazed that he was a partner of all of us. I've also had people say that it's wonderful to see so much love at once.

— White, bi/demisexual woman

Polyamory Gets Better (but Not Simpler) with Age

I came out to my ex-wife and grown children within the last year. I have briefly mentioned on my Facebook page and elsewhere that I am poly. Of course, in the Facebook poly groups themselves, I have great support. In fact, while I have had a polyamorous and serious loving nature since at least eight years old, I was certainly surprised at the number of women who prefer polyamory. It took until I was in my sixties, after divorce from a thirty-year monogamous marriage, to fully accept that my poly nature is not weird, just uncommon. And, being an empowerment coach, I am accepting of others to a greater degree.

I do get the usual guff: "How can you love more than one woman?" "How can you give ALL your heart to more than one woman?" "You're just greedy and it's all about sex." The serial monogamists judge polyamorists while circulating from one failed relationship to another, because one person should never be expected to be the answer to all your needs.

The hardest thing has been to be truly unselfish and unconditionally loving, and then having a woman who said she could accept that I'm poly to suddenly turn on me with "If you really loved me..." because I wasn't jealous of her sexcapades and because I made love to another woman I dearly love as well. I am not a jealous man. I wanted her happiness and safety only. I forgave each confession immediately, because I loved her. The truly heartbreaking thing was that she could never feel loved unless she was my "one and only," despite every effort to treat her like a goddess. She remained the little girl seeking approval and validation from others and claimed I betrayed her, even though I was honest from the start.

While none of my family or my ex-wife and five grown children have been openly critical of my choice, most have simply remained silent on the matter. One son has said that he could see how such an arrangement could work happily and peacefully. When an ex-girlfriend of his needed temporary housing, he and his wife took her in. The experience was very good, with his ex-girlfriend even happily keeping his wife busy while he wrapped a gift for their anniversary. He said they all showed love to one another.

— White, heterosexual man

Chapter 3

COMING OUT TO PARTNERS

For people who have recently arrived at a polyamorous identity, or who have identified as polyamorous for a while but have recently decided to come out, deciding when and how to tell a monogamous partner can be a daunting task. People considering coming out to partners could be well served by thinking through a few of the issues outlined below before embarking on the coming-out process.

It's also important to remember that once you introduce the idea of consensual nonmonogamy into a monogamous relationship, you are changing your relationship regardless of the outcome. You have introduced what Dr. Elisabeth Sheff calls the "polyamorous possibility" and have made you and your partner aware of the potential for consensual nonmonogamy. Once you have granted those words conscious recognition, you cannot take them back. Regardless of whether your partner reacts by thinking they need to "fix" themselves, shuts down, leaves, or agrees to polyamory and moves forward, you can't go backward to a time when nonmonogamy remained unspoken.

Another important consideration is that coming out as polyamorous to your partner has the potential to significantly affect how they see themselves. Your coming out may have emotional and identity implications for your partner that you are not yet aware of. The process of coming out is a balance of risk versus reward.

Before: What to Consider Before Coming Out to a Partner

There are several issues to consider before coming out to a partner, including the risks and benefits, your partner's previous reactions, children who may be affected by the announcement, and special considerations for those already in open relationships who are coming out as polyamorous. If you are certain that your partner will not react well to the polyamorous possibility, you may want to consider whether it makes sense to come out now or to leave the relationship and come out later.

Honoring Your Agreements

If you want your partner to trust you in a nonmonogamous relationship, talk to them about it instead of cheating. Consensual nonmonogamy relies on trust that people will follow through with their emotional and safer-sex agreements. If you start a consensually nonmonogamous relationship with a lie, then you are making an already difficult relationship style even harder. Demonstrate with your actions that you love your partner, are there for them in their daily tribulations, and desire them as a sexual partner. Your announcement/request will go over much better if your partner feels that they can trust you and that you have made consistent efforts to meet their needs.

If it is too late and you have cheated on your partner, you may find that it will take a lot of emotional work to repair the relationship. It is unusual for partners to be able to accept an affair partner as a *metamour*, a partner of your partner, but it's not entirely impossible. Still, you may find that it is harder to rebuild trust with an affair partner in the picture. In addition, if you have chosen to get couples therapy to address an affair, you are likely to hear your therapist demand that the affair partner be entirely let go of.

Risks

One of the primary risks of coming out to a partner is that the partner will freak out and want to break up. Many who hear about a desire for an open relationship will ask if the person who wants to open things up has been cheating and is now trying to transition to a polyamorous relationship. A decision to leave a relationship is especially likely when the coming-out discussion is paired with a demand that the partner open the relationship. Along with the potential to lose a relationship come the myriad impacts of said loss, including an increased risk of financial instability, the need to move residence or even state, possible disruption of children's home life, or need to hire a lawyer to deal with an impending divorce.

Even if the relationship survives the announcement, the emotional fallout can be painful and difficult. The partner who stays might feel very upset, unsure about their new role, or resentful of the recently out polyamorist, who appears to be trying to change relationship rules midstream. That partner might lose trust or feel more distant, or even doubt their former idea of who they thought you were. It can be profoundly disconcerting to hear that your partner is a different person from who you thought they were, which can call for some significant self-evaluation and relationship reevaluation.

Seeking a consensually nonmonogamous relationship can stir deeply held religious beliefs for some people, and the seeker may seem sinful, immoral, or possibly even evil to the religious adherent. Others may take a self-reproachful view, believing that they are inadequate as a person or a lover to meet their partner's needs, and come to view their partner's desire for an open relationship as evidence of malfunction on their part. In short, coming out as polyamorous risks pain on both sides, and it hurts to have that conversation when it's not received well.

Benefits

Given the myriad risks associated with coming out as polyamorous, it is kind of surprising that so many people are doing it. One reason for this rising number of people coming out as polyamorous is that there are also many benefits to coming out.

Many of these benefits are associated with the emotional intimacy that grows between partners as a result of nurturing trust and communication. The best outcomes seem to happen when people are open with their partners before doing something that could harm them both, and when partners trust each other enough to tell the truth. This can also alleviate tension in the relationship if there is a sexual discrepancy. Partners with a higher appetite can find other outlets and don't have to feel guilty for trying to encourage a reluctant partner to have sex or feel sexually deprived themselves, and those with a lower appetite can avoid having sex they don't really want to have without the guilt of depriving their partner.

All this communication and intimacy allows partners to be more authentic and to connect in new and different ways. Talking about what they want from a relationship can encourage people to think deeply about their needs, values, and boundaries. Given free range to discuss those ideas, people can get to know each other on a new level and grow into a new phase of their relationship. It is also possible that the partner who is receiving the news about their beloved's polyamory has already considered the issue independently, and might have even come to think of themselves as polyamorous as well. Alternately, they may have considered and rejected it, which means the disclosure may not be greeted as good news.

Personal fulfillment is a significant benefit to coming out as polyamorous, because polyamorous people can openly structure their relationships to include multiple partners. From meeting new people, to having new experiences and exploring sexual variety, being openly polyamorous comes with an opportunity for personal fulfillment and growth.

Previous Reactions

Another thing to consider when thinking about coming out is how your partner has reacted in other situations when confronted with the idea of consensual nonmonogamy, or any kind of sex and gender diversity. If your partner freaked out watching *Sister Wives* and cried when their friend came out as polyamorous, then you might be prepared for a bomb to go off when you come out. In that situation, take things extra slow and be aware that it may be a really long process. It is also possible that a partner who is deeply monogamous by orientation, religion, or personality may not be able to make that transition. If you are not sure how your partner will react, you can try to feel out what to expect by gently exploring nonmonogamy together in the media. Be sure to see the resources section at the end of this book for recommended media resources that explore polyamory.

Impact on Children

The presence of children complicates polyamorous family life because the adults are not free to simply do what they wish, whenever they wish. As with most parents, polyamorous parents' lives are constrained by the needs, wants, and schedules of their children. When people are in a relationship that includes children, they may be more afraid to come out to their partners or spouses because they're afraid to lose their kids.

This does affect how someone will conduct their nonmonogamous relationships.

Coming Out Polyamorous in an Open Relationship

Sometimes people are coming out as polyamorous in situations that are already consensually nonmonogamous, like open relationships or swinging. In some ways, coming out in an already open relationship is less problematic because there's not an expectation of monogamy. Even so, some people might feel betrayed if they had agreed that there would be no feelings, only sex with no strings. Even people in already nonmonogamous relationships experience jealousy, and just because one form of consensual nonmonogamy works for someone does not mean that another form would work as well.

Coming out polyamorous (with its implications of emotional intimacy and love among multiples) while in an open relationship is further complicated by perceived or actual gender imbalances. Sometimes there is an expectation that men will want or need multiple romantic partners but women won't.

Occasionally people come to discover that their open relationship is becoming polyamorous because someone is developing feelings for an outside lover. This can be especially complicated in gay male culture, where there is frequently an expectation that people will have multiple relationships without developing romantic feelings but often little negotiation around that. Not only does research verify the common expectation of nonmonogamy among gay men, but we both consistently see these issues coming up repeatedly in gay male relationships in counseling.

Cheating

If someone is really a nonmonogamous person and a partner can't accept that, the likelihood of the relationship's long-term survival is low. Is it better to stay miserable in a relationship or try to find some joy? It can depend in part on how well other aspects of the relationship meet the needs of those involved and how well loved one feels in that relationship. The polyamorous community often has a "no cheaters" policy; however, there are regularly extraneous circumstances that make it unsafe for a person to be openly polyamorous with their partner, and so they resort to cheating.

While polyamorous community members generally discourage the idea of cheating and nurture the concept of honesty and open communication, we as a community can be more welcoming of people who are struggling to come to terms with their own identity and face the fears that many of us have felt at one point or another. Sometimes one has to do whatever causes the least harm, and occasionally that isn't what one would expect. Cheating is often the least harmful for the person cheating, but sometimes it is not done or accepted unless there are extenuating circumstances that would result in far more harm to the individual, their family, and their external circumstances. If someone is in a relationship where they are financially, emotionally, or physically dependent on another person, coming out to that person might put them in a vulnerable and potentially dangerous position. We talk in more detail in the following chapters about strategies for identifying the potential risk and harm in coming out to another individual that allows you to identify why someone might look to infidelity in their nonmonogamy. If someone you know is cheating out of fear, it is very important to trust them but also to verify that what they're saying is true. You can help and encourage them to move through this situation that requires them to be secretive. Ideally, conversations about polyamory happen before external relationships start. Ideally, partners would be able to hear each other during these conversations, but it doesn't always work out that way.

When polyamorous people who have the privilege of being out to their partners and loved ones encounter someone who is cheating, those out polyamorous folks should attempt to respond with compassion and education, perhaps suggesting a discussion group or online forum where the person who is cheating can get advice and be in a safe space with people struggling through the same issues. It's understandable that the polyamorous community is hostile, because polyamorous folk don't want to be associated with the concept of sneaking around and lying. If you're in a relationship that includes infidelity or secrecy as a means of harm reduction, trust but verify, encourage partners to be out and open, and if something feels off to you, walk away.

Risk Factors

Some situations make coming out a really bad idea. If a partner has a history of out-of-control anger that includes physical violence or emotional abuse, those issues should be addressed before coming out. This is a particular concern if the partner has a history of jealousy issues. If a partner has already expressed severe discomfort with open or polyamorous relationships it may make sense to avoid coming out if you want to stay in the relationship.

You might want to wait to come out, or not come out at all, if you are at risk from your community. If you and your partner exist in a more conservative cultural space, it is possible that coming out to your partner can be dangerous. For instance, if you have a very conservative family or are engaged with a conservative religious group, your partner may turn to those sources for support after you come out, thus outing you to a group of people who will not accept you. If your partner does not react well to the news, they can out you in any number of ways that could be problematic, such as on social media or to your employer.

After: Responding to Your Partner's Reaction

Okay, you've come out to your partner—now what? There are several issues that people face after coming out as polyamorous, including their partner's reactions and how to best respond. As always, people have their own individual experiences, and you and your partner may feel or experience something significantly different from what we describe below. Your mileage may vary.

Depending on an enormous range of factors, partners can react in several different ways, from complete rejection to enthusiastic acceptance, and everything in between. Some people will have one reaction and stick with it, while others will cycle through several different reactions as they come to grips with the idea of a polyamorous relationship.

Complete Rejection

In some cases, polyamory is just not the right relationship style for that person, for that relationship, at that time, with that person, or in whatever other way it is wrong. Polyamory can be quite intense and demanding, and it is certainly not for everyone. In this case, the partners need to figure out where to go from here, and there isn't an easy answer. If the relationship continues, at least one person has to give up part of themselves.

Shock

Occasionally, people are just not sure how to react to such a major announcement and simply freeze. This "deer in the headlights" response may appear as glassy eyes, distraction, or silence. A similar but louder response to shock is to freak out and scream, cry, or yell. In both cases, shock can produce a strong reaction to unexpected news.

Fixing Perceived Malfunction

Sometimes a partner will interpret a request to open a relationship as evidence that they need to fix themselves in order to be enough for the polyamorous person. This partner might think that if they could just lose weight, get a face-lift, make more money, or be more adventurous in bed, it would reform the polyamorous person back to a monogamist.

Questions

While some people freak out at unexpected news, others respond extremely rationally. Your partner may have many questions regarding what exactly you mean and what a polyamorous relationship might look like. If you know that your partner is an analytical type, be prepared to answer some pointed questions about relationship specifics, not only how you feel about polyamory.

Enthusiastic Acceptance

Some people will have already heard about polyamory and may have been thinking about how to broach the topic themselves, while others will have never considered the idea of consensual nonmonogamy but warm to the idea immediately when they find out about it. If you have one of these kinds of people for a partner, then lucky you! You are going to have the easiest time of anyone coming out to a partner as polyamorous. Be sure to express your appreciation.

Confession and Relief

If your partner has already been engaging in nonmonogamy without telling you, then your announcement could provide the impetus they need to come out about their own relationship(s). Obviously, any cheating will bring up issues of honesty and trust, so be prepared for some conversations around boundaries and vulnerability if a cheating relationship transitions to polyamory.

Strategies for the Fallout

After someone comes out as polyamorous and the initial reaction has faded, life continues, in some ways the same, but in some ways different from before the revelation. Learning to adjust to new realities is an important human characteristic, and it becomes crucial after a potentially significant shift in personal and relational identity. Polyamorous people who have come out can take steps to manage the aftermath of their announcement, and the partner of a newly out polyamorous person can also do certain things to deal with their shifting lives. Both polyamorists and their partners can prepare for some deep and possibly emotional conversations about expectations, safer sex, and reliability, as well as more mundane things like spending money on dates.

Strategies for the Polyamorous Person

There are many strategies a polyamorous person can try when attempting to deal with the fallout of having come out as polyamorous to a partner. These include acceptance, listening, understanding, flexibility, durability, and seeking community.

Acceptance

Polyamory simply is not the right thing for everyone, and you need to be able to accept it if someone says flat out they cannot be in a polyamorous relationship. If your partner rejects polyamory completely, allow them some time to cool off, and work on accepting their decision. They may not remain in complete rejection forever—often people's attitude toward sexual variation does change over time, as their shock wears off and they have time to really think things through or talk with others. However, badgering or pestering your freaked-out partner about polyamory is not going to magically make them want to try it, so give them space for their true reaction, even if it is rejection. It can be difficult and painful to accept, but you might need to choose between being in a romantic relationship with that partner and being polyamorous—not every relationship can or should make the transition into polyamory, and the best people can do is be kind and respectful toward each other while they figure out how to handle it.

Listening

When you are the source of unexpected and potentially disturbing news, be prepared to ride out a bit of emotional turbulence as the announcement sinks in. If your partner is freaking out, give them some space to vent and react. If your partner is frozen, do not take their silence as license to ramble on about how great it is going to be. Instead, attend to body language and provide companionable silence or gentle prompting to see if the stunned partner has any questions. It can be incredibly difficult, but you need to step back and allow your partner space to process this new information without pressure.

Understanding

While a polyamorous person who has just come out might be experiencing relief at freedom from the closet, for the partner of a polyamorous person this unfortunately often means that they go into the closet themselves. The person who has come out experiences relief, but others now have to think about how to talk to their own friends and family members about their beloved's polyamorous relationships. It can be incredibly difficult to know how to talk about consensual nonmonogamy and find nonjudgmental support for the emotional complications that often accompany a transition to polyamorous life.

Flexibility

Be willing to consider other forms of relationship, just as you are asking your partner to consider another form of relationship for you. Flexibility is crucial for polyamorous families, and lasting polyamorous families use it to encourage resilience. There are many forms of consensual nonmonogamy, and if polyamory is not the right one for your partner then it is possible that they might consider one of the other forms. Be open to possibilities and explore new avenues, because going in with a preset view of how things absolutely have to be invites disaster.

Durability

Families change over time when exposed to a sex or gender minority, and sometimes family members who were initially extremely rejecting change their minds and become more accepting over time. If your loved one has an initially negative reaction, consider sticking it out and allowing them time to calm down and reconsider their stereotypes. You can use the time to educate yourself and them, further investigating the advantages and disadvantages of polyamorous lifestyles. This might be a good time to give them a copy of *When Someone You Love Is Polyamorous* by Dr. Elisabeth Sheff.

Seeking Community Role Models

Popular media stereotypes and common wisdom label consensual nonmonogamy as an ill-conceived experiment destined for failure. Absent other examples, it would be easy for someone unfamiliar with happy polyamorous relationships to assume that all polyamorous relationships are flaming wrecks. To counter this assumption, try finding polyamorous community spaces for role models, advice, support, and companionship. The mainstream polyamorous community thrives online and in many major cities across the United States. See our resource guide at the end of the book for ideas on finding a polyamorous community.

Strategies for the Partner of a Polyamorous Person

It can be incredibly difficult to question monogamy, especially if you have a history of issues with nonconsensual nonmonogamy in your own life or in your family. If you have been cheated on or have unresolved issues about cheating on others, then an open discussion of consensual nonmonogamy can be an emotionally draining experience. It can also be an intense experience for people who grew up in families with a cheating parent, especially if that cheating resulted in divorce or family separation. Either way, hearing that your partner wants nonmonogamy can be an unnerving experience, and it is understandable if you find it upsetting. There are a few strategies we recommend for people whose partners have come out to them as polyamorous, including being kind, understanding polyamory as a separate issue, considering your own feelings and boundaries, considering the potential to expand your comfort zone, and educating yourself.

Be Kind

While it can feel incredibly threatening for a partner to bring up nonmonogamy, realize that it is not an attack. Even though it may seem very scary, a partner coming out is a show of trust and an attempt to support intimacy. Give yourself and your partner a break and assume that you both want the best for each other, and then act on the assumption that you wish each other well. It does not mean you will end up doing well together, but you can wish that person well in their life regardless of the outcome of your relationship negotiations.

Remember It's Not About You

A partner's polyamorous identity is not about their partners, but rather about something in them. Just like some people are gay, some people are straight, and others are bi/pan/omni/queer, some people are "wired" to be monogamous, and others are "wired" for nonmonogamy. It would not be anyone's "fault"—and there is no fault to be had—and it is not up to you if your partner is polyamorous or not. You can negotiate agreements about how people act within a relationship, but you cannot change or take responsibility for a partner's polyamorous identity. Similarly, if your partner is monogamous, it is not about you either. They are (probably) not insisting on monogamy just to make you suffer.

Clarify Your Own Boundaries and Feelings

Your partner has just come out to you with this major announcement, so you may be very clear on who they are and what they want. But are you also clear on who you are and what you want? Those important questions should not be lost in the shuffle. Consider carving out the space to look at your own boundaries and priorities to gain some insight into what you really want, independent of what your partner is telling you about themselves. What would be your perfect world if you could have everything you wanted, and what accommodations or concessions are you willing to make in the name of reality? What are your hard and fast limits that you refuse to compromise on?

Do Not Make Agreements You Can't Keep

It can be very tempting in the face of a beloved with an urgent need for something—whether an open or monogamous relationship, a new car, or permission to go to Vegas with the girls—to give in and agree to a relationship you don't want, a car you can't afford, or a vacation doomed to end in arrest and a painful hangover. Even in the face of pressure, it is important for you to hold to the boundaries that you identified as hard limits. If an agreement that your partner is trying to negotiate with you would interfere with a nonnegotiable limit, then it will not be sustainable in the long run. In fact, it will undoubtedly create more drama and pain in the future when it proves unenforceable. Save everyone the pain of a false agreement and say no if you mean no.

Be Open to Trying Something New

If the relationship is worth the effort—meaning that it meets your needs in other areas and is supportive of a positive life vibe for you as a person—then consider stretching your personal comfort zone to include some of the things your partner is suggesting. While this might sound like the opposite of what we said above, it is actually the natural outcome of identifying boundaries. Once you know what you should not compromise on, then you can try being flexible with those things that are negotiable. Obviously, this is a delicate balance that often takes time to become clear, so again please be kind to each other as you learn new things.

Educate Yourself on Polyamory

There are many websites, blogs, chat lists, podcasts, and books on polyamory. In fact, scholars and community members have created a wealth of information on polyamory in the last ten to fifteen years. Some of the books are autobiographical stories about polyamorous people's adventures with nonmonogamy, and others are how-to manuals that explain the ins and outs of everything from ethical communication to dealing with jealousy. The resource section at the end of this book provides suggestions that could be useful for self-study on polyamory.

Respect Privacy

Respect the privacy of your lovers/partners and their lovers/partners. Remember that the content of texts, emails, and conversations are not special fodder to spice up your love/sex life with another, or for comment or opinion by others. In essence, never share such things without the express permission of the other person, on a case-by-case basis. Don't assume a response of "Sure, that's fine" applies beyond a single situation. If your partner's standard of transparency is not the same as yours, rather than violate their boundaries, consider your compatibility. This includes being respectful on social media regarding your relationships and considering how your current partners might feel about you exploring new relationship energy publicly by touching, kissing, or mooning over a new partner. Also, things are likely to change as relationships evolve, and when the rules or boundaries change, inform your partners. They aren't mind readers.

Respect how your potential partner does polyamory. If they want all their partners to be on an even level, or if they want to designate one as a primary, you don't get to tell them that they are doing polyamory wrong or that they should change your status. Come to an agreement and compromise on how you'd like to do polyamory. Sometimes even if everyone is open to a polyamorous relationship, their relationship needs are such that it won't work. For instance, if one partner needs all the relationships to have the same weight and status and a different partner needs their relationship with someone to come before another relationship, then even if everyone is open to a polyamorous relationship it might not work out.

§

Stories: Coming Out to Partners

Kevin Comes Out to Himself

In college, I saw an episode of *Taxicab Confessions* on HBO. There was a guy with two women, and they were all together. It looked perfect to me because I didn't think my girlfriend at the time was...enough. Like I had more love to give and was receptive to more than she had to offer. I had some conversations about that type of relationship, but I never really thought it was possible. I never even bothered to explore it.

Years later, when the woman I would marry, her best girlfriend, and I had an unexpected threesome, I still never considered that an ongoing lifestyle was possible. Only James Bond or someone special like that could manage such an arrangement. So, even though I continued the sexual relationship with that girlfriend, it was still just something quirky about our relationship...not a lifestyle. It was something I did, not something I was.

It wasn't until my future wife began her own outside sexual relationships that I reconsidered what we were doing. The first time she had sex with another man, I was scared about how I would react. She hadn't gotten jealous, but surely I would. I would flip a table and yell at her and call her a bunch of slut-shamey names. When she got home, I asked her for the details and I listened. She told me every single aspect about the guy, the date, and the sex. It didn't faze me in the slightest. I was glad she had fun and, more importantly, I was glad she was home.

It was that point when I realized that if I wasn't jealous and she wasn't jealous, we could keep doing this. We could make this a permanent and enriching aspect of a wonderful relationship. That day, I came out to myself.

— Kevin Patterson, a Black, heterosexual, cisgender man,
    founder of *Poly Role Models*

Tamara Comes Out on Social Media First

I came out as poly to my husband in probably one of the worst ways imaginable. I started by inching toward the BDSM scene. Going to parties, playing with other women with permission, etc. Then I decided I wanted to play with another man. I talked to my husband about it and that was okay with him. I met a guy online who had years of experience in the kink and swing communities. We set up a date at a major local kink event. We had plans to do BDSM play followed by sex. The guy explained after the BDSM play that he needed to beat someone else before we had sex. That person was a regular at his swing parties and therefore somehow had precedence. It was awful. I did not have sex with him. Later at that same conference I was flirting with someone and thinking maybe this could go somewhere when he said something to the effect of "I don't have sex with people I don't care about or have some kind of feeling for." Then he explained polyamory, and I was in. My husband swears I announced I was polyamorous on FetLife before I talked to him about it, though at the time I was convinced I had said something to him first. I have since learned I will often remember having a conversation when I actually had that conversation entirely in my head and not out loud.

Since then we have managed to make poly really work for us. There were a few weeks of hard discussions and confusion, but now we live in a big crazy poly household with four adults, four kids, and a whole host of pets.

— White, Jewish, bisexual, cisgender woman

Jen's Open Marriage Is Working Out

When I initially came out, it was only to my spouse. We were (and still are) happily married. Neither of us had any other partners. I came out to myself at about the same time, over a period of a few years. My partner and I had talked in undergrad about the possibility of having an open marriage even before we got engaged to one another. Neither of us felt that we would last as the other's one and only partner if we were to marry so young, despite loving one another intensely. About a year after we began these discussions, the chaplain fellow at my undergrad asked me and another student what we thought of polyamory. I'd never heard the term before, but I puzzled out from its Greek and Latin roots that it meant "many loves," and I cautiously answered that I thought it would take some pretty special people to be able to deal with things like jealousy, but that it didn't seem like a bad thing. I don't recall what the other student answered, or anything else about that conversation, because my mind was whirling away at what that could mean if played out in real life rather than just as a concept.

It wasn't until a year and a half or so later, after my spouse and I had graduated and gotten married, that it finally dawned on me that that term fit how I'd felt all my life. I'd always been in love with more than one person, and had always felt a bit bad about it, and so I'd done serial monogamy all through my pre-marriage dating years—often dating exes in between new partners, because my love for them had never gone away.

When it hit me that this word fit how I felt, I talked with my spouse about it. We communicated back and forth about it as I began to date someone new, and then as she began to date someone new as well.

Initially my spouse and I both experienced some jealousy. But because we've built our whole relationship on communication and trust, we just kept talking it out, reasoning out why we felt jealous, rather than yelling at or trying to limit one another. I think that's a large part of why we've so far succeeded in our relationship.

The biggest obstacles, aside from jealousy, have been explaining ourselves to people who are very intent on monogamy as the only way to live, and the idea that all partners must be ranked in a hierarchical fashion (we haven't dealt in hierarchies in our relationships).

Being open with my spouse has been a relationship strengthener for us. We've read together and talked together, and we've always had one another to rely upon when the chips were down in other areas of our lives. It's really nice to be loved as I am, rather than having someone attempt to change me or lure me away into monogamy. And now, my spouse and my boyfriend are very good friends (my boyfriend lives with us), my lover and my boyfriend are friends, and my spouse and my lover flirt quite a bit, and we have plans for my lover to move in with us as well. My wife's girlfriend and I talk with one another, too, particularly when my wife is experiencing high anxiety—it's nice to have someone else who cares about my wife to talk with about things like that, and to know that my wife has someone else to lean on as well, to help prop her up when she's feeling down. It's not all perfection— there are jealousy bumps that have to get smoothed out here and there, for example—but overall we've all grown closer as a result of so much shared communication and trust.

— White, bi/pansexual, cisgender woman

Sarah Is More Hurt by Cheating When They Could Have Been Poly

When I was in college, the word "polyamory" had not yet been invented. I was probably about nineteen years old, in an ongoing relationship with my boyfriend, and I fell in love with my best friend, who was female. That was really my first opening up to bisexuality and acknowledging that I was attracted to her. I told her about it, and she said she was flattered but did not return the affection, so for the time that was that. I had also talked a bit with my boyfriend about how I found my best friend attractive and how much fun it would be if we had a threesome or an open relationship. He thought she was attractive too. At the time I felt extremely shy and guilty and bad for having these feelings, so I was never able to really talk about it with my best friend. The three of us had a sleepover one night in the same bed, but nothing happened because we were all too scared to talk about it.

About a year later, after my boyfriend had graduated and had come back for a visit, I walked in on him and my best friend having sex. I was utterly devastated, completely heartbroken. I couldn't understand why they would rather cheat behind my back than have an open connection like I had wanted. I was incredibly hurt. None of us really had the skills to talk it through at the time, and instead I asked my mother for help packing up my room and going home at the end of the semester. She came and kind of dragged the story out of me, and she was furious with the two of them and couldn't understand why I wasn't. She nagged at me to be angry, until I finally said I wasn't angry because I was sad that we were not all three together. She was upset and said it was a disgusting idea and she did not want those people in her house. I did not bring it up again for eight or nine years. Now in retrospect I have a lot more empathy and understanding for my friend than I did at the time. I imagine she felt in a terrible bind in being attracted to my boyfriend but not to me, and she did not know how to navigate that, and therefore ended up having a sexual relationship with him without my knowing. Now I have been in her position, where I have attraction to one partner and not the other, and it is a challenging place to be. I wish we had all had the skills to talk it through back then, but we didn't, and did not have access to any role models. To this day we have not spoken about it.

— White, Jewish, bisexual, cisgender woman

Swinging Girlfriend Not Psyched for Polyamory

I came out first to my girlfriend, whom I had met through a swingers' website. It was before I truly understood what it meant to be polyamorous. I had no experience, and my only exposure to polyamory was through websites. I joined a swingers' website because I thought I did not have time for relationships and only needed the physical and sexual stuff from time to time. Yet my girlfriend and I grew more in love, and she did not agree with the poly lifestyle at all. She understood how I felt, and we tried to mitigate the needs I have. She cried a bit, and I felt a bit ashamed and wondered if I was being shallow or selfish. It has been difficult, especially since we have had to be long distance from each other.

There is a lack of trust from my girlfriend a lot of the time. She thinks I am going to leave her for someone else because she can't meet my needs. Since we have been long-distance she has been of the mindset that I am going to cheat on her, and she always passive-aggressively tells me to be careful when I go out with regard to whom I dance with.

— Latino/Puerto Rican, heterosexual, cisgender man

Chapter 4
COMING OUT TO FAMILY

Because we all come from families with their own degrees of emotional issues already, none of us comes out in a vacuum. In this chapter, when we talk about family we are talking about all kinds of families, not just traditional blood families with two parents. Any issues that a family already has are most likely going to be activated by a member coming out as polyamorous. That can be good—a family that loves and communicates smoothly will probably love the polyamorous person and communicate about any fears or misgivings instead of allowing them to drive the family apart. Families that have a high level of conflict will most likely respond with anger and accusation.

While there has been too little research done to make a definitive statement about coming out as polyamorous to families, research on gays and lesbians who come out shows that although some families completely reject their gay and lesbian members, many come to love and accept them. Even those who initially react with revulsion or rejection can often become more accepting as they calm down and come to see the family members as regular people, regardless of sexual orientation.

What research does exist about polyamorous families indicates that they experience many of the same issues facing gay and lesbian families—disclosure, stigma, impacts on children, finding community, and coming out—except for one. Because polyamory is still fairly new and not as well-known as same-sex relationships, polyamorous families are not as identifiable as gay families. Less recognized, polyamorous families can more easily blend in by allowing others to assume they are a divorced family that gets along well. The polyamorous families that include exclusively same-sex relationships tend to come across as gay rather than polyamorous.

Before: What to Consider Before Coming Out to Family

Coming out to family will be a much different experience than coming out to friends or coworkers. Thinking carefully about why you want to come out, who you're going to come out to, and where you're going to do it can make the process a bit smoother.

Why to Come Out

There are several reasons people want to come out to their families. Emotional intimacy and personal authenticity are important to many people who come out to family members in order to be open and close. Others come out to explain why someone has entered their life and appears to be around all the time. Still others come out because they fear being outed by someone else and want to control the information themselves by coming out first. Sometimes people are outed and then deal with the consequences of their polyamorous status becoming known to others. Sometimes it becomes important to partners to not be kept a secret, and they ask their partners to introduce them to family, or at least let family know they exist. Understanding why you are coming out can help you decide how and when to do it. If you can be close to your family without coming out, consider waiting until there is a compelling reason to come out—especially if you are concerned that they might not take it well.

Another reason to wait is if you are still working through your own feelings about whether you want to be polyamorous. If you have opened your relationship but still have a lot of negative feelings about having done so, then coming out to your family can be problematic. Family will often encourage you to do what is best for you, and if they see you doing something that they perceive as making you unhappy, they may try to encourage you to stop doing it. Also, since many families of polyamorous people have little or no knowledge about polyamory, they may assume that it is inherently bad. As a result, they may try to drive a wedge into your existing relationships or encourage you to change your mind.

Whom to Come Out To

Who needs to know that you are polyamorous? If someone is emotionally close to you and is understanding, they might feel the distance between you when you don't talk much about your weekend, or if you avoid using or stumble over pronouns for the people you were with. Coming out to that person makes sense, because it allows you to maintain an emotionally intimate relationship established through honesty and clear communication.

People who are affected by the relationship might need to know, depending on the degree and type of impact, as well as the characteristics of the person being impacted. An elderly parent who lives in the house will have a greater need to know than a distant cousin who is seen only at family functions.

People whom you know only in passing, know to be gossip-oriented, or feel uneasy about telling for any reason might be better left out of the conversation—at least for now.

Remaining discreet with some does not mean keeping them uninformed forever, and you may decide to tell more or different people as your life and circumstances change.

When and Where to Come Out

To the best of your ability and as circumstances allow, select a low-stress time when everyone has slept and eaten sufficiently for clear thought, people are fairly sober, and you have enough privacy to talk. The location can be anywhere from someone's living room to a hiking trail or a booth in a favorite restaurant—wherever the group feels best. Sometimes an opportunity presents itself spontaneously, so consider now what you would say if you got an opening or if someone asked you directly so you can be prepared with an answer if possible.

Other Considerations in Coming Out

Family relationships often come with financial and legal ties. What are the implications of these factors if you come out to family?

Financial Vulnerability

If you are financially dependent on a family member, it might not be safe to come out to them as polyamorous. Does Dad pay part of your rent? Is Mom putting you through school? Does Grandpa pay for your kids' daycare? Then you are vulnerable to them if they are upset with you for being polyamorous. If possible, gain your financial independence before coming out to family members you think might use polyamory against you or use their financial control over you to require you to change your relationship.

Legal Vulnerability

Sex and gender minorities are legally vulnerable in many ways, primarily in housing, employment, and child custody, and by being subject to selective prosecution for laws that mainstream heterosexuals easily ignore. Polyamorous folks have lost their jobs for violating a morality clause and their housing for having too many "unrelated" adults sharing the same home. They have been selectively prosecuted for adultery and bigamy even when the relationship was consensual and there was no claim of marriage. Possibly of greatest risk to polyamorous families with kids is the potential for an extended family member to sue for custody of children they fear will be harmed by the parents' unconventional relationship style. Preliminary research indicates that polyamorous families are most likely to be sued for custody by an ex-spouse or a child's grandparent, with fewer custody challenges coming from the state.

If possible, insulate yourself with legal protections before coming out. This can be as simple as designating in a legal document who would parent in the event of your death or as complex as incorporating your polyamorous family as a limited liability corporation. Creating these legal documents usually means paying a lawyer, which makes it difficult for working class and poor polyamorous folks to put these legal protections in place. The Kink Aware Professionals Directory is a good place to look for a lawyer who has experience with these kinds of situations.

During: What to Do When Coming Out

Your coming out might be surprising to your family, so it's worth thinking about how you're going to approach the conversation.

Be Selective

There is no need to come out to everyone at once; it is okay to be discreet about your love life with some people and give select others more information. Consider the person's disposition and need to know. People who have proven trustworthy and open-minded in the past are likely to react in kind to your coming out. If someone really needs to know in order to explain some important detail, person, relationship, circumstance, or incident, then consider telling them. Those who don't really need to know for any reason other than curiosity, especially if they are prone to malicious gossip, may simply not be included in the discussion.

It is also okay to share because you are the kind of person who likes to share this type of information. Just make an informed decision, because the more people who know, the more questions that will be asked, and the more additional people will find out by word of mouth. You may find in families with low levels of communication that even if more distant relatives or family friends find out, they may not say anything at all.

Be Calm

Present the relationships calmly, matter-of-factly, and as not that big of a deal. Be sure to use whatever anxiety-reduction skills you have available to help you keep calm, including deep breathing and talking slowly.

Be Positive

Tell your listener what you get out of the polyamorous relationship, why you are in it, and how you feel about it. Ideally, you will feel positively about the situation, as this is your choice.

Acknowledge Difficulties

No one has a perfect relationship, and polyamorous folks face interpersonal challenges just like anyone else. Pretending that you have no problems at all portrays an unrealistic ideal that wise family members will not trust, and they will wonder what you are hiding and why you are pretending. By acknowledging the difficulties you face and talking about how you deal with them, you allow your listener to see your relationship as the multifaceted, vibrant thing that it is. Leaving it to their imagination will inevitably make it appear much worse than it actually is, so take control of the information before they make you out to be a hostage of a cult in their minds.

Be Open to Questions

After disclosing your polyamorous status and offering some reassurance, ask if the person has any questions. If you don't want to have to be responsible for educating your family about polyamory, consider having some books or other educational materials available to give them.

Be Clear

If you are telling one person in a group and not others, be very clear with that person about what they can and cannot say to others. Absent a clear directive to keep the information confidential, the person to whom you have come out might think it is fine to tell other people. If that is truly the case, then there is no problem. But if you want to come out to others at your own pace and time (which may be never), then you need to clearly tell people whom can they discuss it with and who should not be informed quite yet.

What to Avoid

Your coming-out process is *yours*, and you should choose to do it in a way that's comfortable for you. There are some things that you might want to consider avoiding.

Holidays or Big Events

It can be tempting to come out at a family event, because everyone hears it at the same time and you don't have to say it repeatedly or manage some people knowing and keeping it secret from others. While family gatherings can be a good place to draw a select person or small group to a more private setting and come out to a portion of the family, they are generally not the right setting to make an unrelated announcement to the whole group. Shifting the focus of the Thanksgiving feast or Great-Auntie Lareecia's one-hundredth birthday away from the family celebration to your love life is a bad idea. Also refrain from coming out at your sister's baby shower, your mother-in-law's retirement party, or a similar event.

Making it Dramatic

Being heavy and dramatic about the announcement can put others on edge and encourage them to interpret what you say as cataclysmic. It can be hard to stay calm when you are nervous, but take a deep breath and present it with the confidence you want your listener to feel.

Unnecessary Details

Maybe Mom only needs to know that you are being careful, and not the details of your safer-sex agreement with your metamour. Avoid giving too much detailed information, and simply reassure your listener that you are participating consensually and are open to questions—within reason. It is okay to say to people that you are not open to answering something that they ask. It may be a good idea to check in with them about whether they really want all the details of your sex life.

The Appearance of Shame

If you present your polyamorous relationship as something to be ashamed of, then others will think it is shameful. If you really are okay with the relationship, then own it proudly and let others' scorn roll off your back. Those folks who are ashamed or truly not okay with being in a polyamorous relationship should reconsider coming out. Dealing with shame to resolve religious, social, or sexual issues and feel better can be a good thing, but forcing yourself to be polyamorous when you don't really want to be or actually feel very bad about it is a serious problem that will not turn out well for the polyamorous relationship in the long run.

After: Potential Reactions

There are several common reactions that family members have, and anticipating them can help you prepare a thoughtful answer.

Concern About Coercion

Sometimes family members are concerned that their loved one is being coerced into an exploitative relationship by a manipulative lover who is masterminding a harem, and that their beloved is so dim or blinded by love that they fail to notice. Reassuring those family members that everyone is involved voluntarily can help them calm down in the moment, but the best reassurance will come over time as the relationship plays out and they see it augment or detract from your life. Explaining what you are getting out of it and why you chose to try polyamory or identify as polyamorous can help skeptics understand your motivations and accept that you are not being coerced.

This also sometimes plays out in reverse, with family thinking that *you* are taking advantage of the partner or spouse that they are already familiar with.

Slut Shaming

Once relatives accept that you are not being coerced, the next logical step is realizing you are doing this on purpose, which means you want to have multiple lovers (or are at least open to your partner having multiple lovers). In a sex-negative society that uses sex to sell but shames "sluts" (especially women) who like sex "too much," people who admit to having multiple sexual partners simultaneously are ripe targets for slut shaming. Families will sometimes combine coercion and slut shaming in their own minds and think that their relative has been manipulated by a sex fiend: "If that Jezebel hadn't led my sweet son astray, none of this would ever have happened!"

Concern That Your Relationship Is Harmful

Some family members will be concerned that harm will result from your polyamorous relationship. The harm they fear may be amorphous, or it may be directed at their loved one, the children, the family, or society. When someone is concerned about amorphous harm, you can reassure that person that everyone involved is consenting and is free to stop at any time if they do not want to be polyamorous. Emphasize your openness to further questions as they arise, and then demonstrate the true nature of your relationship over time. Like any other relationship, it may be harmful or it may not, depending on how the people involved handle it. Conduct yourself with integrity and compassion, and hopefully your life will demonstrate the lack of harm and even active benefit possible in polyamorous relationships.

Concern for Loved Ones

Relatives may be concerned that polyamory will harm their loved ones in a range of ways, from heartbreak to STIs or social stigma. Talking with them to explore their concerns and explain the strategies you have in place to deal with the issues can help to alleviate their fears. Pointing out that there is no guarantee that you would avoid heartbreak, STIs, or social stigma in a monogamous relationship, and that the same problems are elements of all relationships rather than being peculiar to polyamorous relationships, can help put their fears in perspective. You can also tell your concerned relatives that research shows that older polyamorous people are happier with their lives and relationships than are older people in the general population.

Concern for Children

When first becoming aware of polyamory, many people ask, "What about the children; won't this hurt them?" The answer is "maybe," but no more than monogamous divorced, remarried, or otherwise blended families hurt their children, and possibly even less. Research shows that polyamorous families can provide positive and loving environments for children to flourish into adulthood. That is not to say that every polyamorous family is perfect—they have problems like everyone else, and sometimes their problems are magnified by the number of people involved (though other times those problems are minimized by the helping hands of multiple partners). Empirical evidence clearly indicates that polyamorous families are not inherently problematic and should be given the same chance as other families to be judged individually and by their own merits, rather than deemed pathological simply because they are polyamorous.

You can also point out that fifty years ago, people said that children would be disadvantaged by having parents of different races. The fear of social stigma was reason enough to keep racial lines in place. Now, there are so many multiracial and multicultural people in the United States that "multiracial" appears as a category on the census form. Having members of mixed ancestry is nothing new to American society, but its prevalence and acceptance are products of the last thirty years and only came about because people refused to comply with racist mandates of segregation. Just like stigma has faded from divorced and single-parent families, stigma for polyamorous families will most likely decline over time as well.

Concern for Society

Social conservatives in the United States often cast multiple-partner relationships as the midpoint on the slippery slope from same-sex marriage to the absolute chaos of incest, bestiality, or toasters and cars as marital partners. If the person expressing concern about damage to society holds beliefs deeply rooted in a religious faith that condemns sexuality in general and especially sex outside of marriage, then there is probably no changing that person's mind, and you might be better agreeing to disagree. You can certainly present them with evidence to the contrary, but science is unlikely to change religious beliefs about a range of things, from climate change to sex education, and it is not going to change their mind about polyamory either.

If, however, that person's certainty that multiple-partner relationships would be damaging to society is rooted in social thought and attitudes instead of religion, then you may be able to educate them about the wide range of potential for polyamorous relationships to impact society. Providing them with information can significantly decrease their unfounded assumptions, so consider directing them to some of the resources listed at the end of this book.

Significantly, there are no special disadvantages peculiar to polyamorous families. All struggles that beset polyamorous families are also present in other forms of family, such as divorced, single-parent, multigenerational, or blended families. For instance, children whose families experience divorce, death, or separation have adults who leave their lives in varying degrees, so it is not unusual that some children in polyamorous families miss their parents' partners who leave. Loss is a fact of life for everyone, and learning to deal with it instead of hiding from it can be healthy for children. This does not mean that parents should expose their kids to unnecessary risk, only that there is no escaping loss even if you refrain from polyamory, so learning to deal with it can be a healthy way to manage the realities of life.

They May Actually Be Fine

We have outlined here all sorts of ways that coming out to family can go wrong, but in fact it can also go right. Some families are open and accepting. Some families have a lot of questions but are generally okay with it. Some families just go with the flow, and as long as their family member is happy they are happy.

Responding to Reactions

You can respond to your family's reactions in a number of ways, such as by emphasizing the consensual and careful nature of the relationships, putting the relationships into social context, and using techniques to facilitate communication.

Emphasize That Your Relationship is Consensual

If any of your relatives express concern about your polyamorous relationship, you can reassure them that all the people involved are consenting individuals who are only relating to others who have also voluntarily entered the relationship. No one is being harmed, and society has no stake in what happens in the privacy of people's bedrooms unless it is hurting someone else. As long as the polyamorous relationships are consensual and non-abusive, they should be left to run their course like any other relationship.

Let Your Relatives Know That You Are Being Careful of Any Children Involved

To whatever extent feels comfortable, provide your family members with information about how you are caring for your children's mental, emotional, and physical health in your polyamorous relationships. Inform them, for instance, that you do not leave your children alone with any of your partners until they have been thoroughly vetted and have proven themselves to be trustworthy.

Do you take care to get to know people on a social basis before dating them? Do you see other friends socially and have lovers blend into the scene the same as other adults? Do you tell your children the truth, love them, spend time with them, and communicate to them that they are special to you and you will love them always? Then let your concerned family member know that you are being careful, discreet, and age-appropriate with the children.

Make sure that all adult sexual behavior (beyond simple affection common among friends) is contained by a closed door and the children know what to expect of the adults around them. Above all, make sure your concerned relative knows that there will not be a parade of people moving into and out of the children's lives willy-nilly, because you carefully vet people prior to their entering the family and take time getting to know them before granting them parental status with the children. Even more importantly, follow through with that assertion and really do take time to introduce partners to children or distinguish them from other friends if the children already know them.

Assure Your Relatives That You Are Being Open, Honest, and Responsible

Some people are terrified by the loss of the Judeo-Christian idea that the monogamous family is the most fundamental unit of society. Without that, they wonder, what will keep absolute chaos at bay? How will we teach children the difference between right and wrong? Just because polyamorous families lack the conventional moral basis of sexual exclusivity translated to fidelity does not mean that they have no moral structure or are completely anarchistic. Some polyamorous families do have a religious belief system that structures morality, such as Paganism, Unitarian Universalism, Judaism, or Buddhism, and almost all maintain an ethical structure that emphasizes telling the truth, being compassionate, treating others with respect, honoring fairly negotiated agreements, and taking self-responsibility. Children growing up in polyamorous households are not adrift in a sea of depravity, but instead tend to have clear rules and guidelines that structure adults' expectations of children's behavior.

Remind Your Relatives That Multiple-Partner Families Are Old News

So many societies in different times and cultures have allowed rich men to have multiple wives that polygyny—one man with multiple wives—has been the historical norm, with monogamy being an aberration both across time and even now in global society. In none of these cultures has it also been acceptable to take an animal or object as a spouse, though many allow monks, priests, and nuns to take a deity as a spouse. Polyandry—one woman with multiple husbands—has always been rare and remains much more so than polygyny. If multiple-partner families inevitably led to chaos and social decompression, then it would have happened by now, because they have been around as long as society has been around. Same-sex marriage has not destroyed society, and nor will polyamorous families. Instead, society will continue to change as it always has, and families will evolve with it.

Point Out That Adultery Is Common

People often fail to live up to their promises of monogamy, so even those who say they are in an exclusive relationship like a marriage or a committed partnership sometimes act like they are single and have sex with others anyway. Agreeing to monogamy is no guarantee of monogamous behavior, and at least in polyamory people are honest about what they are doing and can take steps to protect their health with full knowledge of the relationships involved. This can be incredibly beneficial, because cheaters transmit more STIs than do people in consensually nonmonogamous relationships, so it is better for both emotional and physical health to have frank discussions about nonmonogamy instead of pretending to be monogamous.

This one can be especially tricky for people whose lives have been touched by their own or someone else's cheating. If your mom and dad divorced because she cheated on him, then your brother's reaction to your coming out as polyamorous is probably going to be influenced by his feelings about your mother's infidelity and its impact on your parents' marriage. Your best friend, who just broke up with her boyfriend, whom she found cheating on her—again—will almost certainly mix her feelings about her ex-boyfriend with her feelings about your polyamorous relationship. If that person is aware of the concept of projection and how their past experiences can influence their perceptions of current events, then you may be able to have a conversation about how the two nonmonogamies differ and how they are similar, and work through the feelings.

For those who are unable to see or understand the concept of projection, it will appear as if your coming out or existing as a polyamorous person is doing something to them, and in fact doing something wrong in general to everyone around you as well. Much like with people who hold deep religious convictions against nonmonogamy of any form, it will be very difficult to change the mind of the person whose attitudes toward nonmonogamy were shaped by negative events that remain unexamined. Agreeing to disagree and letting the subject drop—at least for now—might be the best way to handle this type of situation.

Use Techniques to Facilitate Communication

There are a few different techniques you can use to manage your life and others' reactions to your polyamory. These include soothing, taking a stroll, educating, allowing time, and setting boundaries.

Soothe
Simply offering reassurance can help a concerned family member calm down and think things through. An initially negative reaction can be eased through calming words and explanations as to the reality of the situation, rather than the fear of what might be. Speaking in a low voice, with soft lighting, and holding a hot drink have all been proven to have calming effects.

Take a Stroll

Walking side by side can make it much easier to talk, especially for two people on an easy stroll. Being able to move and look ahead instead of at the other person will allow some people to relax more and speak more calmly. This might not work well for people with mobility issues, though, so be sure to tailor your strategy to your particular situation.

Educate

Providing information can help family members by increasing understanding and allaying common fears. The resources section at the end of this book lists many educational websites, books, and films, as well as organizations where you can find educational material. One of the easiest ways to educate a family member on polyamory is to give them a resource designed to help non-polyamorous folks understand their polyamorous loved ones, or offer a selection of writings by people in polyamorous families. Books, websites, and other resources provide an easy entry into discussing the realities of polyamory.

Allow Time

Not everything has to be settled or explained in one sitting. Allow the conversation to come to a close after everyone has had their questions answered, or if it continues to circle the same point with no resolution. Taking a break, going home, getting some exercise or food or sleep, and simply getting on with life will put things in perspective and allow initial reactions born of shock to mellow. Time likely will not change a devout believer's mind, but it may well shift others' as they learn and think more about polyamory and interact with their polyamorous loved ones. Some extended families have initially rejected their polyamorous loved ones, only to reconsider later and attempt to rebuild family relationships.

Set Boundaries

If a relative continues to be upset by polyamory and takes it out on the polyamorous people by slut shaming, excluding, attacking, or generally disrespecting any of them, it might be time to take some action. For those who can arrange to see that person as little as possible, limiting exposure can be an ideal first step. It doesn't have to be a big deal or involve a major announcement; you can simply be busy next time they invite you to something or avoid sitting near them at a family dinner.

When a relationship is worth the effort or requires such clarity for other reasons, having a frank discussion about appropriate boundaries and respectful interactions is essential. Explaining precisely what type of behavior has been offensive to the polyamorous folks in the past, with a limited number of specific incidents as examples, is a good way to start. Stating that such behavior is inappropriate and unacceptable, and detailing what behaviors are desired for positive family interactions can help to clarify issues and expectations.

Allow your family member time to respond and to ask questions—this should be a discussion rather than a speech. Be sure to clarify exactly what the consequences will be if the family member fails to treat polyamorous folks with respect: often, refusal to spend time together anymore. Removing yourself or the other person from the social circumstances that allow the negative interactions to occur is generally the preferred consequence for those who overstep the boundaries of polite interaction. This can be especially effective for parents who can limit grandparents' access to grandchildren, though polyamorous parents should take care not to unduly antagonize relatives who may have concerns regarding the care and safety of the children.

§

Stories: Coming Out to Family

Polyamorous Family Run of the Mill for Tamara's Kids

We went poly when the kids were fairly young. Our oldest was five and our youngest was three. In a classic poly mistake we invited my husband's first girlfriend from after we went poly to live with us shortly after they started dating. The kids loved her and were happy to have her around. My son drew a family picture at preschool with her in a sidecar next to the rest of us in the family vehicle. Nobody asked any questions. When they broke up and she moved out just under a year after she moved in, we were worried about the kids. She had agreed to be in touch with them if they were interested, but as it turned out they only occasionally mentioned her and moved on fairly quickly. We had said early on in our outside relationships that if our kids developed a relationship with our partners we would like them to be able to still contact them even if we had broken up. Since then, we have developed a number of close emotional attachments with partners. Often those partners also have children, who in turn become close with our kids. We have a weekly dinner on Friday where we invite our partners, former partners, and friends. The kids tend to run around and play, giving the adults time to socialize with each other. I've been amazed at how close the kids have become over the years and how we have been able to stay close with people we are no longer dating.

About a year ago we moved in with my husband's girlfriend of four years and her two children, one of whom is in college. We've had three kids in the same elementary school with three parents from our house, and my husband's girlfriend's kids' dad, who sometimes comes to events too. We've all shown up at assemblies together and sat together and waved at the kids in unison. We haven't had any questions about it from the school or other parents. We have my husband's girlfriend's kids listed as an emergency contact for our kids, and vice versa. I've been called to talk about my metamour's daughter's trip to the nurse's office, and nobody seems to think twice about it. The school form leaves a space for relationship, and we've just written in "partner." We were concerned that the school would judge us, but now we think that the school may be used to unusual situations, because they have treated our relationships and our family with nothing but respect.

The kids know that we're poly, and we talk about it in front of them, though I can't remember one specific coming-out conversation. We've always been open about it and open to being asked questions about it. There haven't been a lot. We have talked about the capacity for people to love more than one person and the idea that it was okay for them to love one person or more than one person when they grow up. They are eight and ten now.

The only recent conversation about it that I can remember was after the Pulse nightclub shooting in Orlando, when my older son asked if people felt about poly people the same way they felt about gay people. He seemed concerned that we might be attacked. It was a hard question to answer. I told him that I didn't think the hatred was quite as strong, but I also talked about the lack of legal protections around employment, etc.

— White, Jewish, bisexual, cisgender woman

JJ's Sister-in-Law Gets an Eyeful at the *Rocky Horror Picture Show*

Coming out to siblings can be a challenge—or not. My husband, JJ, actually came out to my sister for us. We were all together at a *Rocky Horror Picture Show* concert we had put on, and JJ was with a date, whom he introduced to my sister initially as a friend. I was on stage performing, and JJ leaned over to tell my sister that we were polyamorous. Later that night JJ told me that he had told my sister because he didn't want her to see him making out with his date and feel alarmed that he was cheating on me. It ended up being a big nothing and really liberating; she didn't care and was clear that she still loved us, and I felt lighter having the

secret out there.
— White, heterosexual, cisgender woman

Irene's Polycule is a Mix of Out and Not

About two years ago, our girlfriend and her three kids finally moved in with me and my husband, and we decided it was time to confirm what we were pretty sure everyone knew anyway (except for her family, who are very religious and a bit closed-minded; they still don't know—at least she hopes). My husband is not very close with his family—we have been together for fourteen years, and my birth family has definitely become his "real" family. The family members that did matter to us were very open and accepting; others weren't. But my family loves our girlfriend—her kids are just a few more grandkids to my mother. We have told her oldest child. He is sixteen. There are eleven-year-old twins, and they don't necessarily know, but the time is coming. They have to have a clue. There are a few gay family members in my very large, close family, and everyone is always so accepting, I really wasn't scared to come out and just say that we were polyamorous, and I am so glad I did.
— White, bisexual, cisgender woman

Mike Comes Out to Select Siblings

Initially, I came out to my youngest brother, the sibling I am the closest to. A wonderful guy, my brother is smart and funny, with savage wit, and will say anything to anyone. If anyone was going to be accepting of this it would be him. The first time we kind of talked around it: when my now ex-wife and I were hanging out with him, I mentioned to him that we had opened up our marriage. He said, "really?" but we discussed it no further. Half a year later I had separated from my wife and was living in a bachelor pad. Talking to my brother on the phone, I told him how much more I had embraced polyamory and explained whom I was seeing and what kinds of relationships I had. He asked if my ex-wife was doing this too, and I said she was not interested in sex with emotional connection but more in sex with people she didn't know and had no emotional attachments to. She wanted to see only other married men who would not get attached to her. He asked if I was happy, and I said I was not sure how to answer that question, because my marriage of twenty-plus years had imploded.

I knew he shared everything with his wife and asked him to hold this one back so we could discuss it more fully at a later time. My ex was not doing well after the divorce, partially because we didn't have any friends in our marriage. She never wanted to expend the energy to keep up with friends, so when we broke up she had no one to talk to. My ex-wife began to lean on her relationship with my sister-in-law (my brother's wife), and one day on the phone my ex-wife spilled the beans about me being polyamorous. At the time I did not know, and it was not until months later when I was visiting my brother that he told me that his wife knew because my ex-wife had outed me. I was upset, because I had wanted to take my time and do it right, not getting her on the phone to talk to her about it. I had planned to speak to her in person during my Christmas visit, and it never worked out, but I was still planning to talk to them myself later.

The last time I was in town visiting them, my sister-in-law asked me to come with them to see their daughter, who was waiting tables in a restaurant, and it was mostly deserted. Seeing my opportunity, I said that I knew that she had probably heard that I had poly relationships and that I wanted to talk to her about it. She was interested in hearing more about it, so I explained that there was more than one person that I was close to. She asked about the sex, and I explained my web of relationships and how the people I see also see other people.

She asked if the kids knew, and I said yes, that we all hung out at this wonderful Friday dinner party with kids and adults sharing food and community, talking about what was happening in our lives. It gave me a sense of community that I have experienced only a few times in my life, a sense of comfort and fulfillment that

I had not felt in years. I expressed my sadness and regret that she had found out from my ex-wife and that I was not able to tell her myself. I said that I was not trying to convince her that it was the best way for her, but it was definitely the best way for me, and it was making me whole and healthy, and not hurting anyone. The whole conversation lasted about forty-five minutes, with her asking (occasionally prurient) questions and me answering as honestly and fully as I could. Ironically, it all sounded absurdly Victorian, because my main sweeties advise me about (and can veto) any of my other loves, and if one of them says she thinks it is not a good idea then I usually listen, because she is right. We talked about jealousy, freedom, love, marriage, honesty, and learning. At the end of the conversation she said she thought it was a screwy relationship type but did not judge me for it. She said she was not sure if it was exactly the right way to be, but added, "If you're happy, then stay the course. Your brother and I love you and we will always be here for you, no matter what."

All in all, everything came out fine, and even though it was thoughtless of my ex-wife to expose that personal information, it gave me the impetus to finally bring it up with my brother's wife.

I am happy that my brother and his wife were so accepting of me, because they are the last family members I will tell until my mother dies. It makes no sense to bring it up with her now, and none of my other family members are open-minded enough to even want to know about it.

— White, heterosexual, cisgender man

Sarah Kind of Flubs Coming Out to Her Parents

This is, in some ways, a story of how not to come out. I had spoken to my parents about my interest in alternative relationships when I was in college, and the reception was not so great. In 2001, I was in my late twenties, and I had been in a triad relationship with a man and a woman, and was living in Washington, D.C. My parents had not met either of these people and did not know about the triad. They knew about my male partner and were really excited to meet him when they came to visit me in D.C.

We all went out to dinner, and my female partner was there as well, but as "just a friend." After dinner, she left, and my male partner and I went back to my apartment with my parents to chat. I said there was something we wanted to tell them, and my parents at that point thought I would be saying that my male partner and I were going to get married. Instead, I came out with the fact that we were in a triad with the woman they had met at dinner, and my parents got extremely upset. My father—usually the calm and loving one—basically accused my male partner of dominating and controlling me and asked how I could do this, and said that it was terrible. They left, and we did not speak for a month—much longer than usual, because at that point we usually spoke every few days.

Little by little, communication started up again, and even though my parents got upset about my forays into unusual relationships or sexuality, they would usually come around when they saw I was happy. Communication improved over time, and about a year later my entire triad visited my parents in their home, and we were welcomed. Since then I have been very open with my parents about being poly, and they have been extremely supportive and have even joined me at some local Loving More events in my hometown.

It became clear to me that I had not managed their expectations—when I said that my male partner and I had something we wanted to discuss with them, their minds went to marriage, and it was extra shocking to hear that I was in a polyamorous relationship. It would have been easier if I had not set them up to expect a marriage talk and if my male partner were not there when I told them. If it had just been me and my parents, then I think they might have felt less defensive.

— White, Jewish, bisexual, cisgender woman

Mom Values Midnight Rose's Happiness

I was living with two men. My mother, who was sixty-seven at the time and lived in North Carolina, knew of one of them, and when I talked to her about my activities, I would just say "we" went to whatever it was. She also knew I was friends with the other man. But I was unhappy attributing all my happiness to one person when two were actually involved. I went home for a visit, and while I was there, I sat her down at the dining table and told her that I was actually living with, and in a relationship with, both men. She had a lot of questions. At the end of the conversation, her final words were, "If everyone knows what's going on, and everyone is happy with it, and *you* are happy, then I guess I'm okay with it." A few months later, she had surgery, and all three of us went down to help take care of her for a few days. She appreciated that.

— White, bi/demisexual, cisgender woman

R Sets Some Clear Boundaries

Shortly before Christmas a few years ago, my father wrote an email to me and my eleven siblings about an Iranian Muslim friend of his who had four wives. I responded back—and copied my siblings—saying I had two partners. Some of my siblings already knew, and two of them had already met my girlfriend, so it was time to come out to the entire family.

In the email, I explained that my then-wife and I had agreed we wanted more than one partner before we married. My father wrote back asking some prurient questions. A few of my siblings said they were okay with it, but never asked for details. My oldest sister wrote back, saying she didn't understand how her siblings could condone adultery and that just because my wife agreed to it does not make adultery acceptable. My wife replied to my sister saying she supported my relationship with our girlfriend. That didn't convince my sister, and she continued to send emails to me and others condemning me for not living by her values.

I wrote back saying that if her only contact with me in years was to condemn me, then I did not want to hear from her again. I told her I would program my email software to send any emails from her directly into the trash. In my last email to her, I set a clear boundary. If she wanted a relationship with me, she would have to ask somebody else to relay messages to me, or she would have to convince one of our relatives that she was truly sorry for what she did. I have not heard from her since.

— White, heteroflexible, cisgender man

RV Road Trip Disclosure

I recently decided to tell my dad I was poly. I have a second serious relationship now, and I wanted to give my newer partner the same place in my life as my longer-tenured partner. Also, since my mother, who never would have been able to handle the news, passed away eight months ago, telling my dad became an option.

My dad and I had planned a two-week 1,800-mile road trip in our RV. I decided this would be a good time to have the poly talk. I spent the first half of the trip waiting for the "perfect time" to transition to the topic in conversation, but I realized, of course, that such an opportunity was unlikely.

Following dinner one night, spurred by that realization, I said, "So, I have two girlfriends." Just like that. My dad's reaction was basically just to ask how that worked. We had a good conversation, where I explained what polyamory was and how, specifically, my brand of poly worked. He handled it extremely well, better even than I had hoped.

— White, pansexual, cisgender man

On the Way Home from the Vet

I sort of came out to my mom as poly at one point. We were in the car, coming back from a vet appointment with my cat. For whatever reason, I had been talking a lot about both of the women I was dating at the time, but not outright saying I was dating either of them. Their names were Kyla and Lindsay.

Finally, after a while, my mom asked, "So is Lindsay your girlfriend?"

I hate my mom knowing too much about my love life, so I was reluctant to talk about, but I confirmed that she was.

My mom's response was more or less "Oh, that's nice."

She waited a few beats and then suddenly came out with, "So wait...is Kyla *also* your girlfriend?"

And I was pretty much sitting there thinking *Oh shit, I didn't know that I was being so obvious.* So I lied and said, "Umm, she used to be."

My mom asked, "So was she upset when you broke up? Is she jealous that you're dating Lindsay?"

And I was like, "Well no, she's not upset. She introduced me to Lindsay."

That seemed fine with my mom, and we either sat there quietly for a little while or moved on to some other subject; I don't remember.

Now, like I said, I don't really like my mom knowing too much about my love life, but I also don't like lying, so eventually I went out on a limb and admitted, "Yeah, actually, Kyla is my girlfriend, too."

So again, she wanted to know, "Is Lindsay okay with that? Is Kyla okay with that? No one is jealous?"

"Nope, they're good friends, and like I said, Kyla introduced me to Lindsay, so I think she kind of had it in mind that we might end up dating."

So, my mom, being a very conservative, fundamentalist Christian, responded, "Oh, well, I don't have any problem with that as long as no one is having sex with anyone."

And, you know, since I was definitely having sex with both of them, but had no intention of telling my mom that, I let the subject change pretty quickly.

I never used the word "polyamory" with my mom, but I talked pretty openly about dating both of them for a while. At first, she seemed pretty okay with it; then eventually it seemed like she

was getting uncomfortable with it, so I stopped talking about it.
 — Matt Bear-Fowler, White and Indigenous progressive
   Christian pansexual, genderqueer creature

Sara's Dad Wings It and Ends Up Doing Great

My dad found out that I was bi when I was fourteen, and that I had two partners when I was seventeen. He just said, "Hey, be careful when it comes to sex." He doesn't always understand it. He doesn't know how to interact with Amanda, the third in our triad. My parents are really awesome about having holidays together and giving gifts to our partners and even their kids. The biggest thing is feeling lost about what they should do. There are no scripts for how to behave in these situations. When I was with women in the past, he used to treat me like I was "the boy." He will bring cookies for Amanda. He even got her a sack full of candy last time he came to visit. He makes an attempt to be supportive, but he still feels lost. When I was younger, he felt like he should screen my partners and tell them never to hurt his daughter, and that sort of thing.
 — Sara, White-dominant-identified, bi/pansexual,
   cisgender woman

Octavia's Polycule on Trial

With regard to being out as poly, my family has been through a real trial with my husband's girlfriend's divorce. She and her husband had been in an open relationship for some time. He was the first to have sex outside of their marriage. He had agreed to what they had done. Still, when he filed for divorce, my husband, his other girlfriend, Jane, and another friend, Jackie, were all summoned to give depositions. The depositions all had numerous questions about their sex lives. Their FetLife profiles were printed out for the opposing lawyer to use as evidence.

The lawyers asked things like "Do you kiss in front of the kids?" "Do you have sex with the door open?" "What do you do in front of the kids?" and "What would you do if your daughter became involved in this lifestyle?" The lawyer clearly knew nothing about polyamory. Jane was able to do some good advocacy, saying things like "Like monogamous people, we don't have sex in front of the children." Still, it has made our whole family afraid. My metamour's husband is still trying to stop her from bringing her daughter over to our house for dinner or to play with our children, who have really enjoyed spending time with her and ask why she can't come over any more frequently.

— White, bi/pansexual, cisgender woman

Spring Break Smackdown

Right before Easter of 2012 I had a huge fight with my mom. It was the new year when I actually came out as poly to her, and I was dating Kirk (who has a wife, and at the time had two other girlfriends). After that, my mom talked to me about it all the time and kept pushing the issue: "How are things going; are they going to go further?"

She had known about my boyfriend, but she did not know about the dynamic with my boyfriend. So for four or five months she had known about him, and kept asking me for more information about him: "Who is he? What does he do?" It kept coming up about whether he and I were going to get married or move in, what kind of commitment we anticipated forming. Finally, I explained that we were poly and he was married. At the time she seemed to take it very well. "Everyone knows?" she asked, and I said, "Yes, we are open about it." On the surface she seemed good, and I was thrilled, surprised and happy that there seemed to be no judgment. Initially, it went smoothly.

My birthday is in January, and my mom wanted to buy two tickets to a show in town, for me and whomever I wanted to take. I said I would take Kirk, and she said she could not buy the tickets because she couldn't condone my relationship with a married man, and buying the tickets was tantamount to endorsing it. I said, "Fine, if you don't want to, then don't." She said she would just have Dad buy them so she would not be party to "it." Very judgmental. By early February I had gotten sick of the snide comments and told her it hurt my feelings that she judged me and made irritating and passive-aggressive or outright aggressive comments.

She responded, "You can do what you want; I just don't want to know about it."

Over the next couple of months she made underhanded comments like "He's not really your boyfriend" and made snide remarks constantly. Finally, the week before Easter, it was spring break, and I was going to take a vacation with my best friend for a few days and then my boyfriend would come to meet me too. My mother was going to take care of my son, because I had not been on a vacation without him in years. When I told her I was going on vacation with my best friend, she kept asking, "Who are you really going with?" over and over, until I said, "Why are you asking questions you don't really want to know the answer to?"

She responded, "I knew it! You are lying to me!"

"No, I am not!" I responded. "I just left out the part you told me you didn't want to know about!"

We proceeded to hash it out, with her saying things like "There was no way you could be happy living like this," "I guess I wouldn't mind so much if there weren't children involved," "Why can't you just get your own man?" and "I just hate seeing you act like a whore and a slut." I responded that Kirk's wife had her own boyfriend, she knew all about it, and no one was cheating. Even though I had told her before that we were open about it, she did not really understand that the first time, and it finally sunk in during the Spring Break Smackdown. She ended the conversation by reminding me that she loved me and no one else would ever love me like she did. I responded that she may love me, but she did not like me at all, and if I weren't her daughter she would have nothing to do with me. That shut her up, because she realized it was true and she had no response to that.

Two weeks after the Spring Break Smackdown, I was having dinner with my dad, and he mentioned the fight I had with Mom.

Dad said, "My philosophy is, I don't care if a man has sex with six women and a goat, as long as it's not my goat." After that, he reassured me that as long as I was happy and being treated well, he couldn't care less what kind of relationship I had. Parenting done right!

Over the next six months Mom started paying attention to how Kirk treated me—helping me move into my place, being more supportive of me than other men have been. Finally she remarked, "He really is the Superman of all boyfriends—I have seen him treat you better than couples who have been married for thirty years."

— White, heteroflexible, cisgender woman

Awkward Coming Out to Mom Goes Well

My wife and I each had another partner who did not live with us. I came out to my mom rather awkwardly, and through her to other people (because Mom always talks about her thoughts and feelings with someone she's close with). By that point in time, I'd been living openly polyamorously among my friends, but not around my family. I felt pretty awkward about it around my mom, because I've always told her everything. My teen years were pretty rough with her, but since then we've become friends, and I hated lying by omission to her all the time.

So when she and my stepdad came to visit, I waited until he wasn't around (he wouldn't have understood) and then asked Mom if we could talk. And I told her that my spouse and I had an open marriage, that we had other partners. She was quiet, and then she said, "Well, it's your life." And she hugged me. I was surprised, because I'd expected something like "How could you do this to [spouse]?!" But there were no accusations. She didn't say anything else about it at that time, but it was a relief to know that she knew.

At first, Mom was convinced that my being polyamorous meant I had to be something other than heterosexual. I had to explain that while I was bi/pansexual, that had nothing to do with my relationship orientation.

I also had to deal with Mom outing me to other people. I knew then (and know now) that she didn't mean any harm by it. It was just a new concept with her, and she had to talk about it with other people. The only way she knew how was to talk about how her daughter had come out to her. Fortunately, she kept it in the family.

She did ask me not to tell my stepfather, which was okay with me. None of my family (my whole family aside from him knows now) has wanted to deal with explaining it to him or with the not-so-smart remarks he might make about us. My mom has been very accepting of the partners she's met. She regularly asks after their well-being and asks questions about things she doesn't quite understand. I feel really lucky to have such a fantastic mom.

— White, bi/pansexual, cisgender woman

Kevin Finds the Right Wife, but His Mom Doesn't Like It

When I met my wife, I fell in love with her almost immediately. I knew I'd marry her after our first date. A big part of why was because I could tell her anything and everything. With my ex-girlfriends, I felt like I had to walk on eggshells and tell them what they wanted to hear. With my wife, I could say whatever I was thinking and we'd address it as maturely or humorously as the circumstance determined.

A few years ago, well into my marriage with my wife, I tried to come out to my mom. I said, "You know, my wife and I date outside of the marriage. I do my thing, and she does her thing." My mother wasn't interested in hearing about that at all. I realized that I didn't really have a whole lot to say at that point, because I wasn't really dating anyone seriously and didn't know what direction my ethical nonmonogamy was going to take. I told her I wasn't going to bring it up again unless I had a legitimate reason to bring it up.

Years went by, and polyamory became less about what I was doing and more about who I was being. I started seeing someone seriously who went from being kind of a hookup with no boundaries to sort of a stepmom to my kids, someone who lived with us every couple of weeks. At that point I couldn't ignore how big a role she was taking in my life. I couldn't pass her off as a friend, and I wouldn't pretend that she didn't exist.

So I went back and told my mom, "You know, this thing I tried to tell you about years ago, well it's more serious now. I'm not just doing this, I'm talking about it, writing about it, going to Meetups, meeting people. I'm part of a community, and this woman is not just my friend, she's a girlfriend, she's part of my family." My mother still wasn't interested in hearing about this, so I kept trying to have conversations and kept getting brick-walled. I bought books, I sent YouTube videos, I sent articles. The only response I got was "I don't want this around you and your family, I don't want this around your children, I don't want to be in a room with this person," and I can't deny that someone in my family is a part of my family.

The thing about my polyamory is that everyone I'm around decides their own level of involvement. If you want to be a part of my life and I can accommodate you, I can make that happen. If you don't, there's nothing I can really do about that. I am hoping my mother will eventually come around, but I'm not holding my breath. Every once in a while, I'll still send her a resource. I was featured in a newspaper article recently, and I sent her a copy of the article with a letter pleading for her to be a part of my family, but I haven't heard anything back, so that's where it stands.

As for my kids, it sucks. I grew up a country away from my grandparents on my mother's side. I had to hop on a plane to see my grandparents, and my kids' grandparents live just two hours away, but they can't see them at will because Mommy and Daddy dare to love more people than their grandparents would've liked. I'm not going to put my kids in an environment where their parents aren't welcome, where their grandparents might say something to slight us or somebody my kids love, whether that be me, my girlfriend, my wife, or anybody else that's a part of our lives.

My mother said she was not the only one in my family I was making uncomfortable with my polyamory. She wouldn't tell me who it was, and I'm not going to guess, but I will distance myself. I've spent a lot of my life trying to be a really good son, cousin, and nephew, and if this one thing that's different about my life versus their own is enough to drive me out, then it tells me more about my family than I wanted to know.

— Kevin Patterson, a Black, heterosexual, cisgender man and founder of *Poly Role Models*

Marcia Makes a Mistake

When my third daughter was a few months old, we went to our church to have her christened. My whole family was there—Mom, Dad, aunts, uncles, siblings, nieces, a nephew, my wife, and our older kids—as was the entire congregation, our pastor, and everyone else in town. At least that was how it felt once Marcia began to speak. In truth, only half the town was there.

Marcia and I had been dating for six months at the time, and she had joined us for church once before, going out for brunch and then playing croquet afterward. My family knew her but did not know that our relationship was polyamorous, or that my wife not only knew about but even approved of my relationship with Marcia. It never occurred to me that I would need to tell Marcia not to announce our polyamorous relationship to the entire congregation, because it never occurred to me that she would even think of such a thing.

It seemed like Marcia had been waiting for the time when the pastor would announce that anyone who objected should speak now or forever hold their peace. The pastor never said that, because it was a christening, not a wedding, and certainly no place for her to suddenly speak her mind. So when she stood up and cleared her throat, I thought she was going to make a toast or something, which was weird because no one was drinking, seeing as how we were all there for the christening ceremony and all. I gave Marcia a look like *What are you doing?* She gave me a thumbs-up and then launched into her declaration that we were polyamorous and she was my girlfriend—yes, that kind of girlfriend. You could have heard my jaw drop in the stunned silence that followed, and then the pastor cleared his throat and completed his benediction over my infant daughter. Still struggling to grasp what had happened, I locked eyes with my wife, and we telepathically agreed that we had to batten down for the shit storm that was on its way.

Most of the people at church never said boo about it, but my mom and dad were another story. Not only did they not say anything about it, they didn't say anything to us at all for months—just cut us off completely. My wife thinks that we never would have heard from them again if not for the lure of the grandchildren, who ultimately proved irresistible. Eventually they broke down and returned one of my phone calls, and we went back to a cold and rocky relationship that took years to recover. We have never brought it up again, even though we have had other partners—some of whom my parents have even met.

And Marcia? Let's just say that was not her last surprise, but almost. It became readily apparent that I could not trust her or maintain a lasting relationship in which she respected boundaries and common sense. She didn't understand why I was upset or how I could see her announcement to my family, friends, and faith community as anything but joyous. I pointed out that we should have talked about it beforehand and chosen a very different time and place, and she said she was moved by the beauty of the ceremony and wanted to share our joy with our assembled community. It was a good instinct, in a way, but incredibly poorly executed.

— White, heterosexual, cisgender man

Michael Doesn't Need to Come Out to His Mom

My mother was not polyamorous sexually, but she was one of these people who had a variety of intense connections among many different people. There were literally a hundred people I knew as my aunts and uncles growing up, and eventually I realized that many of them were not actually related to me by blood. At some point in my early teens it dawned on me that there were about fifty cities in the United States where I knew someone well enough that I could walk into their home and they would feed and clothe me. So when I eventually developed radical connections among multiple lovers, it did not seem like a big deal to anyone. I never actually even came out to anyone; I just lived my life with multiple partners, and my family welcomed them. My mother was a vital woman who collected amazing people, and her example led to me build my own web of amazing people, and it simply seemed natural to everyone.

— White, heterosexual, cisgender man

Pleasantly Surprised by Religious Parents

After being with our girlfriend for over a year, my husband and I decided that it was time to come out to our parents. I stressed about it for two days. My father is a pastor, but even so, my parents are fairly open-minded. All I could do was keep playing back in my head a conversation I had with my dad ages ago. He had said that he understood gay and straight, but he thought people who were bi were either confused or didn't want to make up their minds. I have always been really close to my parents, especially my dad, and I lost two days' sleep playing over how this whole conversation might go.

Finally, the time arrived, and I called my mom. She listened for a minute, and then interrupted and said, "It's okay. I mean, we kind of knew. You didn't have to tell us. As long as you are happy, we are happy for you. It's not really a new thing." I remember heaving a sigh of relief and crying. I couldn't believe it was done with and it was okay! Both of my parents just accepted it and started including our girlfriend in talk of our family. It was far from perfect, but I have to give them a lot of credit for being open to listening and accepting all of us.

My mom has struggled in relating to our girlfriend, but I don't see that as any different from struggling to relate to a monogamous partner. There have been a few weird comments about our sex life that I basically answer with the fact that it isn't really anyone's business, and that tends to work well for us.

My parents were proud that I was willing to be myself and open up this part of my life to them. It is awesome for us all to do things as a family when my parents are in town without anyone feeling left out.

— White, pansexual, cisgender woman

JJ Is Not Sure How (or If) to Come Out to His Brother

My brother used to live in Europe, and when we became polyamorous I didn't feel moved to tell him, because he was far away and it didn't really come up or matter at that point. Recently, he moved back to the States with his wife and their two kids, and suddenly we live just a few hours apart. Thinking about telling him is tricky, but it's actually for reasons much more about his personal life than mine. He is very personally conservative and has strong feelings about infidelity, based on some things that happened in our extended family and the ways in which it directly affected him while we were growing up. Given his experiences, I am very concerned about how opening up about being poly might affect our relationship.

So up to now, we have refrained from telling him. However, pretty much all of our friends know that we are poly, so if my brother and his family hang out around us at all they might hear about it from someone else. So we probably should tell him. But I am afraid to tell him in case he freaks out. At this point, I am just not sure what I am going to do.

— White, heterosexual, cisgender man

Not a Concubine

I no longer interact with my oldest sister. My father speaks as if my ex-girlfriend were my concubine rather than my girlfriend.

He sees male–female relationships in traditional patriarchal terms. One of my younger sisters told me she wants an open relationship, but her husband does not approve.
— White, heteroflexible man

O's Sister Changes Her Mind

I was in an open triangular triad, where the three of us were all in a relationship with each other.

Shortly after my triad formed, I told my sister about it. In an angry voice she said, "When are you going to grow up?" We didn't talk about it again for ten years, when the triad split apart. She found out about the split from Facebook: one of my partners had posted that she was moving out. My sister contacted me and said she'd come to accept my partners and liked them, which was news to me.

Things were awkward and weird for years. After about six or seven years she seemed to start to accept it, but never said anything. So it was only slightly less awkward and weird. She still doesn't know I have other partners. I guess she assumes I have only two partners, and I don't see any reason to enlighten her.
— White, pansexual trans woman

(Custody) Battle Royale

I came out to my mother in a very awkward way. I had been staying in the closet, but I became pregnant and wasn't sure which of the men in our triad was the father. I finally told my mother several months into the pregnancy. I hemmed and hawed for a bit, and she finally asked me point-blank if the man I hadn't been out about being with was the father. I told her he might be. I told her the three of us were in a relationship together and were planning a ceremony to publicly commit to each other and celebrate our relationship. She made me promise not to tell anyone in the family. She said that she was afraid it would give my grandmother a heart attack. I agreed, reluctantly.

We had our commitment ceremony in early November, and my parents spent the weekend visiting family several states away. I consoled myself at the time that at least I knew they wouldn't be there so I wouldn't spend the whole time watching the door for their hoped-for arrival. Because of my promise to my mother, I couldn't invite two cousins (who were also some of my best friends) to be with me on the day.

On Thanksgiving, my parents were at my aunt's home with about half the family. I called to wish everyone a happy Thanksgiving. My grandmother got on and told me she was praying for me and "my friends." That's how I learned that after making me promise not to tell anyone, my mother had told two of the worst gossips in the family, spreading her version of our relationship. I tried sending a letter out to the family to clarify and reach out so people would understand and hopefully welcome my partners. Some of the family did try to understand, but many just cut me out of their lives.

My parents got more and more obsessed with our relationship over time and used my being out as poly to set child services on us, and then sue for custody of our children. I had to get a court order to get them into family therapy with me. Once in family therapy they asked me if I planned on forcing my daughter (who was five years old!) to sleep with my lovers. Apparently they never listened to a word I said about consent, about ethics, about chosen relationships, and just jumped from multipartnered to "forced polygyny" to "child marriage" without bothering to stop at "No, our daughter may do some weird things, but she would never hurt her children that way."

There have been other things, like getting kicked out of an apartment for having "more than one family" living in it, but that was the big one.

Aside from my family, everyone has been at worst concerned but also supportive and often highly supportive. I've run into curiosity, a lot of people saying "I wish I could do that," etc.

— White, bisexual woman

Biological Parents Were Polyamorous Too

I was adopted as an infant, and I got to know my biological parents in my early twenties. When coming out to my adoptive parents and the family I was raised in turned into a disaster, I was terrified of coming out to my biological family. But I wasn't going to hide who I was from them. So I called, and I got my mother and father on the phone at the same time. And I said, "This is what's going on."

They immediately expressed concern—but not for any of the reasons I expected. It turns out they had been a triad for a while and that relationship had ended badly—badly enough that the third member of their triad apparently never fully recovered from it. So while they fully understood and supported my wanting to be polyamorous, they were afraid I was repeating their mistake.

In a way they were right—it was a supremely unhealthy relationship. But they never wavered in their support for me or for my right to choose my relationships; they welcomed my partners into the family. And when that relationship did fall apart, they never blamed it on polyamory or told me I should admit that monogamy was better. They just supported me through it, and when I got involved with my current live-in partner, they told me I made a much better choice this time. Having the full support of my biological family has been huge, including their welcoming me and any/all of my poly partners to come visit and/or live with them if we can ever afford the airfare.

— White, bisexual woman

Chapter 5

COMING OUT TO KIDS

As with almost any polyamorous situation, there is no one-size-fits-all way to come out to children. How and when you come out depends a lot on the age and temperament of the child, and the situation of the family. The general best practices for coming out to kids are to tell the truth in an age-appropriate way, avoid providing too many details, and let them ask questions.

Consider the child's need to know before telling them something that could become a burden to them if they end up having to keep it a secret. Kids who interact with partners routinely obviously have a much greater need to know who those adults are and their roles in the family life. New, casual, or long-distance partners who may not be figures in the kids' lives can probably remain anonymous, unless there is some reason to tell the kids about them.

One of the primary motivating factors that encourages parents to come out to their kids is the desire to maintain open, honest, and close relationships with their children. Hiding something big like a serious relationship out of necessity introduces a degree of falsity and deception that can create emotional distance and encourage kids to keep secrets too. Open and honest communication helps parents and kids stay close, something that many polyamorous parents value. In some cases, however, it can be difficult for children to have to keep one parent's secret at the expense of lying to another parent.

Before: What to Consider Before Coming Out to Kids

You know your children better than anyone else, and you're in the best position to decide what they need to know about your relationships. Thinking about the following factors can help guide you in making that decision.

Age of the Child

As any parent knows, a child's age shapes their developmental stage and their ability to understand social situations. While young children have only a rudimentary understanding of adult relationships, teens and adult children are generally able to understand complex motivations, interactions, and negotiations.

Young Children

Young children almost always take their family form for granted and do not understand the complexities of adult relationships. Instead, young kids tend to understand the adults in their environments in the context of what the adults do for them—reading them stories, playing on the floor with toys, allowing them to play dress-up—rather than how the adults relate to each other. They don't need a lot of information about what goes on after they go to bed. If the child is used to adult friends being around for social time, then they may not need any explanation that differentiates those adults by sexual status, which the kids don't really understand anyway.

Tweens

Older children in polyamorous families begin to understand that their families are different because of their increased awareness of the rest of the world and exposure to others. The rarity of polyamorous families in the media alone would tip off any curious twelve-year-old that things are different in their own family, and exposure to peers' families would most likely confirm that most people are single, monogamous, cheating, or divorced.

If a child notices differences and is the kind of child to ask the parent(s) questions, then it is best to sit back and wait for the kid to bring it up. Some parents might want to bring it up with children in specific circumstances. For instance, inquisitive children who listen to adult conversations and watch adult interactions might sense something is going on and wonder why the adults are hiding things. Initiating a conversation with that curious child might reassure them that there is nothing to be ashamed of and allow them to ask questions they may not have previously been able to articulate. Alternatively, a child who fears that one parent is cheating on the other can find great comfort in knowing that the parents know about and have agreed to the relationship.

Because it will gross them out completely, kids generally do not need or want sexual details about the adults' relationships and will most likely be fine hearing euphemisms like "hanging out" or "spending time together" rather than explicit labels like "lover."

Teens

Teens might notice something is happening and feel uncomfortable about bringing it up, so be prepared to cautiously bring it up with them if they have not already broached the subject. Some teens will have figured it out and not want it spelled out for them, and a few might be surprised. Because teens understand sex to a much greater degree than their younger siblings and are involved in their own sexual awakening, they will probably be more grossed out about their parent(s) having sex than a younger child would be.

Adult Children

Adult children have most likely established their own lives and had their own romantic experiences—all of which can influence the ways in which they interpret their parents' polyamorous relationships. Some children will cheer their parents on, glad to see them blossoming and enjoying their lives. Others will be aghast at their parents' impropriety and refuse to interact with multiple partners. For those with unresolved issues about infidelity—either their own or their parents'—this could be an especially unwelcome announcement. Similarly, adult children who practice a religion that condemns polysexuality (and usually any other form of sex that is not between married heterosexuals with the potential to make a baby) will most likely greet the news of your polyamorous relationship with stoicism or even alarm.

Type of Family

What your family looks like and how you came to polyamory can make a big difference in your children's perception of your relationships.

Polyamorous from Birth

When children are born into polyamorous families or their parents form polyamorous relationships while the children are very young, it is often best to wait until the child brings it up to introduce the idea of polyamory. Once kids start asking questions, that indicates their thinking has become sophisticated enough to make group comparisons and notice differences in their families. When the child does ask questions, answer them with honest and age-appropriate information, and ask if they have more questions. Let the kids know they can ask more questions in the future if new ones arise.

Blended After Birth
For older children whose families transition to a polyamorous configuration, it can be better for the adults to come out to the kids so the kids don't think the adults are cheating on each other. These kids don't need to know the details of any sex or romance; they just need to know that the parents are open and honest about it with each other and the kids, and that the kids can ask questions about it.

Who Else Needs to Know

Children born into polyamorous families might not need to be as circumspect about their families as would kids from divorced families with a nonpolyamorous parent who might sue for custody if they found out about their ex's polyamorous relationships. Even kids born into polyamorous families can have a grandparent or other family member who could become upset about the polyamorous nature of the family

In addition to the child's age and need to know, polyamorous parents should consider the potential impact of the child blurting out information to someone who may not know of the polyamorous family. Young children do not understand which topics should remain private, and may occasionally say things that adults would rather they kept to themselves. Giving a small child information that could be damaging to the adults and then expecting that child to have the discretion to know when not to talk about it is unrealistic. At the same time, you do not want to give the impression that being in a polyamorous family is a shameful secret the child must hide.

All children need to know the boundaries around whom they can talk to about their polyamorous family. If parents want the children to avoid telling grandparents or clergy about the polyamorous family, it is crucial that the parents help the kids distinguish between shame and discretion. Some polyamorous parents use the analogy that it is okay to be naked at home, and going from the bathroom to the bedroom nude is not a problem because nakedness is private and home is private so it is okay. It is not okay to be naked at school or in the grocery store, however, and even small children can understand that being home is private and being out in the world is public. The same goes for talking about the polyamorous family at school—it is a private thing best left at home. Similarly, the same way we do not say certain words (e.g., swear words) in front of Grandma, we also do not talk to her about the polyamorous family, because she would feel uncomfortable about it and we don't want to be rude. Be sure to tell the child that the family is fine, loving, and safe for the child, and that being discreet does not mean being ashamed. All of this without making a big deal out of it! We realize it is a tall order, and that parents who tell their kids the truth in a supportive, compassionate, and age-appropriate way are generally doing their best, which is probably pretty good.

Stories: Coming Out to Kids

Annie Almost Comes Out to the Kids

When my son was nine or ten he was clearly wondering about my boyfriend. After working up his courage, he eventually asked me, "Are you at that point with each other that you have seen each other in your underwear?"

Later that same year my kids were sitting on the couch watching *Hannah Montana*, and in that specific episode Hannah had to choose between two guys that she liked. After the episode, I pounced on what I saw as a teachable moment, thinking I could introduce the idea so that when I was potentially partnered with multiple people at some future point we would have already talked about it some. As usual, we were talking about what we saw on the screen with a critical eye toward thinking through plot points instead of just accepting them. I asked the kids, "Why does she need to choose at all? If they know about each other, then it is fine; she can have both of them, just divide up her time."

My eleven-year-old daughter responded with shock: "No, Mom, that's just wrong. She has to choose!"

My son was awestruck by the idea and responded, "Whoa, that's brilliant! That way if one does wrong, you still have a spare!"

That day set the stage for me to talk to them about polyamory for years to come.

— White, bisexual, cisgender woman

Pat Realizes Her Daughter Already Knows

When my daughter Susie was growing up, she and I went to this summer solstice festival together every summer. The festival was a little like a sex-positive Pagan hippie summer camp with lots of different people, some of whom were polyamorous. One summer we were hanging out at the festival having a discussion with some other folks who mentioned that they had multiple partners. Susie got angry, declaring that cheating was wrong.

I said, "People are not possessions."

Susie responded, "Not everyone can be a bi poly Pagan!"

I was floored—not only that she knew all of those words, but that she applied them to me. At that moment it became clear to me that I would not have to come out to Susie at all; she in fact understood quite a bit of what was happening around her.

— White, bisexual, cisgender woman

Tamara Is Open Without Telling a Lot

My kids have basically grown up in a poly house. My husband and I opened our relationship when the kids were three and five years old. We didn't have an explicit conversation about polyamory with the kids, but they noticed that we had friends around and that we were more cuddly with some than others. We also had some friends who slept over and some who didn't. When the kids were curious about this, we just said, "Mommy and Daddy have sleepovers with their friends just like you have sleepovers with your friends." When our first outside partner moved in, we didn't really talk with the kids about what that meant. We mostly referred to her as a friend.

As time went on, my husband and I both ended up partnering more seriously with people who had kids. Our partners and their kids would come over together or sleep over, and often the kids interpreted events as our setting up playdates and sleepovers for them and not for our own reasons. Now, in situations where our children have become friends with the children of our exes, we continue to invite those families over so our kids can maintain those connections.

Last year, my husband's girlfriend and her daughters moved in with us. Unlike the first time one of our partners moved in, this time we sat down with the kids and had a talk about becoming one big family and what that meant. Even in that conversation, I don't think we used the word "polyamory." My husband and his girlfriend now share a room, and I have my own room. At first the kids were concerned about this change, thinking that maybe it meant there was some problem in our relationship. We explained that we were just relating to each other differently but we still loved each other and weren't breaking up. It didn't take long for the kids to adjust to this as the new normal.

In talking to our kids about love and relationships in general, we have told them that it is okay to love people of any and all genders, and it is okay to love one person or to love more than one person. We try to leave things open for them to make their own decisions about what their love life will look like in the future.

— White, Jewish, bisexual, cisgender woman

Kevin's Curious and Clever Kids

I did and didn't come out to my kids. They're young enough that anything we present them with is their norm. I didn't come out and say, "Hey, Mommy and Daddy love different people as well as each other." Instead, they started noticing familiarity between me or their mother and other people who were at the house. Then, when nobody was looking, they would corner those other people and say "Hey, do you love my mom/dad?" which of course would lead to some awkward responses. We never lied to them; they just figured it out on their own.

It was their norm, and having grown up in schools where there were lots of same-sex parents, lots of interracial parents, lots of kids who were adopted, or, like their dad, first-generation Americans. They've already come across so many diverse family structures that our family structure didn't faze them at all.

The only time I really "came out," if it even counts, was when I showed my older daughter a newspaper article talking about my polyamory blog, *Poly Role Models*. She's only six years old and was really excited at the prospect of her dad being famous. Which I'm not. But she asked me what my blog was about and why it was popular, why people were looking at it. I explained it to her; I explained polyamory and what my blog was about.

I was able to use the movie *The Book of Life*, which she had just watched five times straight and is about a love triangle, as a reference for polyamory. I was able to use the fact that we love both her and her little sister the same as a reference. Once she heard me explain it all from that standpoint, she was just fine. She raised her hands up, yelled, "I love my family," and went back to playing. That's probably the last conversation I'll have to have with her about it until she starts dating herself.

— Kevin Patterson, a Black, heterosexual, cisgender man and
founder of *Poly Role Models*

Chapter 6

COMING OUT TO FRIENDS

Initially applied to gay people whose families of origin had rejected them, the idea of "chosen family" has become so popular in the past fifty years that it is verging on mainstream. Chosen family members are often friends and current or ex-lovers who decide to bond and rely on each other for extended periods of time. They stand in contrast to biolegal families, or those that are related through a shared lineage (consanguine) or a legal relationship like marriage or adoption. People are born into biolegal families of origin and sometimes create chosen families from scratch as they make their way through life.

Sometimes, for people coming out as polyamorous, this chosen family can be the hardest to tell. Many budding polyamorists fear that their friends will leave them behind, shun them, or continue to be friends with them while issuing subtle barbs that call into question the validity of their relationships. Given the level of hostility toward unconventional sexualities and religious condemnation of sex for fun, polyamorists who are nervous about coming out to friends have good reason to consider their announcement strategy carefully.

Before: What to Consider Before Coming Out to Friends

There are important things to consider before coming out to people whose relationships you value. It probably makes no difference to come out as polyamorous to the Uber driver who raises eyebrows at the number of people smooching in the back seat, because that person has no influence on the rest of your life. Your lifelong friend's reaction, in contrast, can make a world of difference to your daily life.

Why Come Out?

Once they've come to terms with the fact that they're polyamorous, many polyamorous folks will eventually want to come out to their friends. People come out to friends for a variety of reasons, especially intimacy, honesty, and recognition. Emotional intimacy can be extremely important to polyamorous folks, and it is a feature of human nature that when we love someone, we want to be close to that person. If you are hiding an important part of yourself, then it can be quite difficult to be truly close while being so evasive. Coming out as polyamorous can open avenues for support, understanding, and acceptance among friends who have shared other life experiences already.

Sometimes people already love more than one person and don't want to hide that anymore, because hiding means lying, which can go against polyamorous values of honesty and integrity. Not only is lying uncomfortable for some polyamorous folks, but it can also be painful for the partner who is concealed, because it implies that something shameful is happening, that others in the relationship are ashamed, or that the partner should be ashamed of themselves. Because concealing a relationship takes a lot of effort, creates emotional distance, and can hurt people who are hidden or deceived, polyamorous people generally come out to friends in an attempt to be honest, close, and loving.

Why *Not* Come Out?

People can be completely freaked out by consensual nonmonogamy of any sort, and can use that to damage others who are unconventional. The harsh truth is that polyphobia and sex negativity in general are real and have real consequences for people in the bedroom, classroom, and courtroom. Possibly even worse, prejudices like mononormativity (the assumption that all legitimate relationships are and should be monogamous) are most evident in social networks because they can directly influence the way friends treat each other.

Consider the Risks

Before opening yourself to the potential rejection that can follow coming out as poly, consider your risks. When thinking about coming out to a friend, it is wise to consider how much influence that person wields in your world.

- Does this person have power over you in some way? Are they your boss who could fire you or your friend who owes you money, or do you owe them money? Even if they don't have a material hold on you, can this person hurt you if they are unhappy with you?
- How have they reacted to sexual or relationship variations before? What do they think of gay people, sister wives, and bisexuality? Have they expressed sex-negative or intolerant views in the past, or are they fairly open-minded about sexuality?
- What are the potential consequences for you if this person reacts negatively? How much influence do they have over

your emotional and physical world? How has this person used their influence with others in the past?

- Can it wait? Is there some event or conversation that is likely to out you soon and you want to talk about it before someone else outs you? Can this wait until you are less vulnerable or you know more about how they might react?

Considering the possible risks and consequences of coming out can help to clarify whether it is worth it at a specific time. If your friend who has made a few homophobic jokes in the past is letting you live at their place for free, maybe hold off on coming out as polyamorous to that friend until you are living in your own place. If you put a lot of emotional energy into your chosen family and are not very connected to your biological family, then the fallout can be much greater and much scarier. People with lifelong friendships may well fear the ripple effect and how it will affect their friendship circles.

Consider the Potential for Judgment

Even those unable to fire or ostracize can still hurt with judgment. The fear of contempt and allover ickiness that comes with judgment is one of the main things that keeps polyamorous people from coming out. If friends react to disclosure of polyamorous identity with scorn, it has the potential to spoil the friendship. People who are considering coming out rightly fear the potential for rejection and loss of relationships that may result from negative judgments against their polyamorous relationships or lifestyle.

Consider Their Experiences with Cheating

If you are coming out to a friend who has had their own experiences with cheating, it can influence the way they react to your desire for or experiences with consensual nonmonogamy.

When someone has unresolved issues about their own cheating or being cheated on, it can color the way they view polyamory. This experience with cheating does not have to be direct; for example, those whose parents cheated can also have strong reactions to nonmonogamy in any form.

Take Steps to Prepare Yourself

Doing a bit of groundwork can help to aid in the process of coming out. There are many ways to come out to your friends and loved ones, and they are often different for each situation. Tamara suggests feeling people out slowly, dropping hints before coming out, because it can allow you to get a feel for how someone might react. Rebecca feels that it's better to rip the bandage off quickly—that way you can mentally prepare yourself for any fallout rather than slowly leaking.

During: What to Say and How to Say It

Say whatever comes to mind and feels most natural. Most importantly, be clear that you are simply providing information and that you are not coming on to them. At least not right now.

After: Strategies for Dealing with Friends' Reactions

In some cases, announcements of polyamorous identity or lifestyle are met with open acknowledgement and warm acceptance, and those tend not to require a lot of strategy other than celebration. At other times, the feared judgment and rejection become a reality. Sometimes people freak out, and sometimes friendships end. If your friends react with distaste and rejection, remember it is not the end of the world. While losing a friendship can be painful, it provides some consolation to note that losing someone you can't be honest with is not as bad as losing a true friend who loves you for who you are. You can't be close to someone if they don't know who you are. The choice is really between having a surface-level friendship with someone who doesn't know you, having a deep friendship with someone who does, or not having a friendship at all.

Stay Calm

Many people who come out to friends find that although they need support from their friends, they often end up needing to support friends who are unpacking their own feelings surrounding monogamy and relationships. This effect can be amplified when friends have had experiences with cheating and are having trouble differentiating between consensual nonmonogamy and cheating. It's important to remember that you're not in charge of your friends' feelings. You cannot control their feelings, and you're not responsible for their feelings. You are only in charge of your reactions. If a friend is having a negative response, you can be there to support them, but keep calm and remember it is not about you. If you feel that the situation is escalating more than you are comfortable with, it may be best to step back from the situation and allow them time to process their feelings independently. Regardless of their reaction, it is important to take care of yourself and your emotional needs first. Friends will need to come to their own understanding of your relationships, but you can try to explain your situation and the difference between polyamory and cheating. You may end up losing a friendship if they are unable to tell the difference or accept you as a polyamorous person.

Be Positive

Remember when you're coming out to friends to avoid framing polyamory like it's some horrible thing they're learning about you. Instead, treat it like it's something positive, and talk about how much joy it brings you. If you treat it like a horrible thing, your friends are more likely to react as though it is horrible. People often take cues on how to react to news based on how you share it. If someone is excited for you and wants to learn more, they may want to be a polyamory ambassador. (We'll talk more about that later.)

Be Clear

Many people fear that someone coming out as polyamorous is coming on to them or their partners, or that polyamorous people don't respect monogamous relationships. Even if they're supportive of polyamory, they may be put off by the idea that "all the rules are broken" and "everything is fair game." Not everything is fair game, and it's important to help friends realize that you support their monogamous commitments to each other and are not trying to bully your way into their relationships. A good way to support your monogamous friends is just to be specific about your intentions: "I am sharing this with you because I want to be honest about who I am, not because I'm interested in you or your partner." It is okay to talk about how polyamory is a stellar life choice for you, how it has increased your joy, and how your relationship style simply works for you better than monogamy may have. Talking about your happiness is great! Take care that you're not forcing your polyamory and your ideal on anyone else.

How do you know if there's a polyamorous person at the party? Don't worry; they'll tell you.

Avoid Being Preachy or Snobbish

If you are coming out because you want a relationship with a friend and/or their partner, the best advice is to move slowly. Make sure to leave space for people to process the new information, and don't talk negatively about monogamy. If you want people to respect your relationship choices, you need to respect theirs. If someone tells you they aren't interested in poly, don't talk about how polyamorous people are more enlightened than monogamous people. In fact, don't say that to anyone. Polyamory is a valid relationship style for many, many people. So is monogamy. One is not better or worse than the other. They are simply different.

When someone asks you to not preach the gospel of polyamory, try to respect that. There should be a space for you to talk about your life freely, but that doesn't mean always talking about how polyamory is a superior choice. Be aware that being out as a polyamorous person can encourage some people to be nervous about you being alone with their partner.

Take Heart and Create Community

You may have to build your support network before coming out if your only existing support network consists of the friends who don't know you're polyamorous. If you don't have partners, building that support network is crucial. Even if you do have partners, do not underestimate how important building a support network can be for your well-being and the durability of your relationships. Ensure that you have active self-care practices, and remember that losing a friendship does not mean just acknowledging the loss of friendship, but also grieving the loss. It will not last forever, in the same way that the pain of a breakup does not last forever.

§

Stories: Coming Out to Friends

How (Not) to Be a Polyamorous Ambassador

I came out to my friend, who took it as permission to go on her own sexual adventures, but she did not do it safely. She would meet up with people she'd met on the Internet and have sex in their cars. Somehow she heard me about the poly stuff, but she didn't hear me about the safety stuff.

The polyamorous community wants to make sure that when you're talking about poly and being poly openly, you encourage safety and consensuality. You don't want to encourage someone to cheat on their partner because they felt that you gave them permission by living your life. Encourage talking to partners *before* opening up, not later. Post about safer-sex things (like sti testing) and encourage safer sex and consensual behaviors in a positive, light way. You may not intend to be "sex positive" or part of any group that talks about sex and relationships, but if you are becoming a beacon of permission, there is some responsibility to foster healthy ideas and behaviors to keep yourself, your friends, and your community safe.

If you don't want to be a poly ambassador, tell your friends about Google. It is not your job to educate, but many people you're coming out to will have had no experience with poly people before, and you are their first impression of the entire community. It's a huge responsibility that not everyone wants to take on. If you're not able to shoulder that responsibility, having a few links or suggestions for where your friends can go for answers is a tremendous help.

If you do want to be a poly ambassador, that's great! It's worth doing to make sure that people really understand your lifestyle. Keeping open-ended wording is great. Try not to give over-whelming generalizations about the poly community, as those tend to carry over with the small amount of media about poly people and can lead to a large misunderstanding of polyamory and polyamorous people.

If you want to be a poly ambassador, speak from your own experience. Talk about your own life, talk about what worked and didn't work, and don't pretend you're perfect, because you're not. Make sure you're reading up on poly media and websites so

that you know what you're talking about.
— White, pansexual, cisgender woman

Jen's Ongoing Coming Out

I have come out to friends in different ways and under different circumstances. Usually I've casually mentioned other partners to my friends to test their reactions, and if there are questions, I've followed up. This has been, for me, the most ongoing form of coming out, because I'm always meeting new people and making new friends.

There are a few people who've chosen to keep their distance after learning that I'm polyamorous. I've had a few people accuse me of being greedy or of not being able to make up my mind or of being codependent. Of course, I've heard the first two about being bi/pansexual as well, so I've grown used to hearing those things. A few people have asked me how I thought God felt about my being poly (I'm a theologian and Christian), with the implication that God wouldn't think terribly highly of the idea.

I've strengthened some friendships via being myself. I'm more comfortable being "me" when I know that people know all of me—that I'm bi/pan, that I'm poly, that I'm progressive and Christian. It makes me able to be more open when I talk with people, and that in turn tends to make them be more open and comfortable with me.

I've also become some people's go-to person for questions about relationships, sexuality, and gender, which I don't mind. Sexuality, gender, and theology are my main areas of study, and because of my multiple relationships, I feel more able to listen openly and without judgment to others' questions and concerns. Some friends have come to me to critique popular culture and systems of power, too, which I love.
— White, bi/pansexual, cisgender woman

High School Best Friends Say "No Way"

We told my wife's two best friends from high school. The three of them had been friends for over ten years. My wife attended their wedding. They told us it was an immoral lifestyle and would only ruin people's lives. They then told her to never contact them again. It has been eleven years, and when my wife heard they had a baby, she sent them a card. They didn't reply but asked a mutual friend to tell my wife to stop contacting them.

— White, pansexual trans woman

Platonic Trio Turns into a Duo

In college I had two best friends, Naomi and B, who shared most of the same classes with me. We got close as a result of late-night smoke breaks outside of our dorms and last-minute study sessions where we would edit each other's papers. My fondest memories of that part of my life are spending time partying and hanging out with them. We were nearly inseparable, and often covered for each other or shared the cost of gas for driving the two hours into the city to go dancing at the gay bar.

After I left college, I found myself in a relationship where I loved both my current partner and my childhood love, and was not comfortable choosing between the two. I was in a tough spot, but luckily, the three of us decided that nonmonogamy would be the best option for all of us. I didn't tell Naomi or B about my nonmonogamy right away, as I didn't want to lose my friends or have them judge my relationships unfairly. B was pretty chill about life in general, so I wasn't really concerned about her. I figured she might not get it, but she'd be completely on board with anything I did. Naomi, on the other hand, was what I can only describe as "rabidly monogamous," so I knew I was going to have to handle that delicately. About a year or so after I got married, I realized I'd have to share that part of my life with B and Naomi, as I was starting to have some very serious relationships. There were very few people who knew about the polyamory already, and I wanted the support and love of my besties.

Because B and Naomi had stopped speaking to each other, I had to call them each separately and gently talk around their own argument. There was good news though, because B took it so well! I was so thrilled that she was on board. She didn't quite understand it, but she said she loved me, supported me in my relationships, and wanted me to be happy. Naomi did not react quite that well. She was upset, and almost angry at the fact that I stopped seeking my One True Love to accept that maybe I had Many True Loves. I firmly told her this was non-negotiable, and she could either support me or not. She begrudgingly accepted to be in my life.

Fast-forward to a few months later. B and I had a bit of a falling out where she said that she would always love me and never judge me, but didn't actively support my lifestyle. I couldn't understand how you could claim to love someone and never judge them, but not support them. Not supporting me in this instance was much the same as judging to me, and I was heartbroken. Over a year after that falling out, we spoke one more time. I haven't heard from her again.

At the same time, Naomi was starting to come around, as she began to see how nonmonogamy suited me. She saw my relationships play out and began to understand how I could feel comfortable in this relationship. Most importantly, she saw that it made me happier than I'd ever been in the time she'd known me.

Now, four years later, Naomi and I live close to each other and are closer than ever. It did break my heart to lose B, who was basically a sister to me, and I still miss having her in my life. Recently, a friend of mine told me that rejection makes a space for the right people in your life. That friend was right. I now have a huge, supportive family, and amazing people in my life who love me. Not only do they love me, but they also actively support me. It was really hard and truly hurt to lose someone I loved, but it didn't hurt to lose someone who didn't love all of me. I know I deserve to have people who love me for me.

— White, bisexual, cisgender woman

Tamara Is Out All Over, Even When
She's Not Even on the Date

I've come out to all of my friends. I'm out on Facebook. I talk about my life with pretty much everyone. It's kind of hard to miss. None of my friends have told me I was wrong or bad or anything like that, but a lot of my older friends have sort of drifted away over time. For some I think it's because my life makes them uncomfortable. Sometimes it's me. I've found over time that I hold back from my friends who are not poly. I'm worried about making them uncomfortable or feeling judged, so I just don't spend as much time with them as I do with my poly friends.

One particular experience we had that was really odd was when my husband was on a date and ran into the parent of one of our son's friends. She came up to the table and started talking to him, without realizing that his date was not me. When she realized, she was sort of surprised, and then wandered off. As a result, we decided we had to come out to her, and if we were going to come out to her we should probably come out to the parents of my son's other close preschool friend. My husband agreed to watch the kids while we three moms went out to dinner. When we were out, I explained the situation, and also that our "friend who lives with us" was my husband's girlfriend. They were a bit surprised. The woman who had run into him on the date said she actually didn't think much about it and hadn't been worried that he was having an affair. They both seemed to be of the opinion that they could never do that, but they were okay with the fact that we did. They've continued to invite my son to get together over the years and have come to our house.

— White, Jewish, bisexual, cisgender woman

Tyler's Second Chance

Early in my time as a poly person, a good friend of mine from college, Tyler, came to visit. I was in grad school and had been with Vanessa, the woman who would become my wife, for several years. We had decided to try polyamory and had just begun to come out to our friends. Unfortunately, we did a bad job of explaining it and picking the time to come out, and Tyler was one of first people we told. He just assumed that something bad was happening and that Vanessa was taking advantage of me, and that this was going to be a really bad idea. Tyler was supposed to stay with us, but instead he stood up and walked out, saying that he could not be party to this. Vanessa and I were surprised and sad to see him go, but we got over it and moved on.

About five years later, Tyler wrote me a letter apologizing for the way he had reacted. Tyler explained that he had worked through some personal issues and realized his reaction had a lot more to do with himself than it did with us or our relationship. He wrote that he wished he had spent more time talking to us and trying to understand the situation. He said that he regretted the time lost in our friendship and did not expect us to forgive him.

Of course we forgave him. Tyler will be in our area in a few months, and we are going to hang out with him. Our friendship, once lost, has been repaired, or is at least on its way.

— White, heterosexual, cisgender man

Kitty Loses a Friend While Creating a Family

I don't know that polyamory was the only reason they drifted away, but I definitely lost some friends when I started coming out to people as poly. My best friend's sister is a really open-minded person, and I had no fear about coming out to her, because I thought it would be no big deal to her. When I told her, I was on the phone with her while my partner, JJ, was driving. We were going to see her at a party the following night, and I just blurted it out, that we were poly, thinking it would be no big deal. To my great surprise, she reacted very angrily and yelled at me, saying that I wasn't around as much as I used to be, and that when I was around I was distracted. If polyamory was the reason that I had not been around, then she didn't like it. I was stunned, and it took me a moment to gather myself and formulate a response.

Rather than being distracted with polyamory, I was grieving my mother, who had died just three weeks before. My father had died five years before, and JJ and I had just found out that we were infertile, and my dreams of motherhood were shattered. Not only was my family drastically shrinking, I was having a mid-life crisis of identity, wondering who I was without motherhood, without my beloved parents, and without my high-powered corporate job that had proven ultimately unsatisfying. It had been an onslaught of losses, and I had been spending a lot of time alone crying. I had put myself in a vulnerable position coming out to her, and she attacked me.

Polyamory was actually a way for me to begin to rebuild a family after losing my parents and my potential for motherhood, not the source of my distance from her. I was really hurt by her reaction, feeling like she kicked me while I was down, grieving my mother's death, and that I had expected her to keep loving me no matter whom I slept with. We are still kind of friends a little bit, but not like we used to be. The distance makes me sad, especially because I considered her part of my family then, but definitely don't now. She is a mom, and it made it extra hard that she did not understand the way I was creating my family too.

— White, heterosexual, cisgender woman .

Lorrae's Friends Just Don't Get It

When I first came out to friends, people thought it was going to ruin my relationship and destroy me. One friend in particular asked rude questions like "Which one are you going to choose?" and "Which one do you love more?" I had to learn to silence those voices and surround myself with more supportive people.

It's been a year, and I've been poly successfully, and my partners are all getting along. All of my friends have come around and are not judging so much anymore. It may be because I live in such a liberal area of Philadelphia. I've had friends in monogamous relationships come to me and say "This looks awesome" and "We're thinking about trying this too." Some of my friends have felt like my coming out was beneficial in that it gave them an opportunity to see this as a possibility. I feel surrounded by a supportive community now who understands.

— Lorrae Bradbury, a White, heteroflexible, cisgender woman
    and founder of the website *Slutty Girl Problems*

National Coming Out Day and Many More

I was in a loosely defined open relationship the first time I came out. The second time, I was single. The third time, I was in an open polycule.

I've come out a few times over the years, usually in casual ways, and have met with casual skepticism that this kind of life-style could work. One year I shared it in a Facebook status on National Coming Out Day (as a follow-up post to one reminding everyone how very, very queer I am). I normally just casually mention it to people as part of a conversation about a relationship I'm in: "I was hanging out with my partner and their wife—oh, yeah, I'm nonmonogamous, so my partner has other partners, and everyone knows about everyone else. Anyway..."

My mom doesn't really seem to understand, and continues to think I'm dating everyone my partner is dating, or that I'm dating nobody and we're all just a group of friends. It can be difficult to introduce to people you've just started dating, or on a first date, but online dating takes care of that issue pretty easily.

I get lots of opportunities to talk about polyamory to people, and to gush about how much love and joy I get to experience in my polycule, with lots of people going "Oh! My friend so-and-so is poly too! You should meet them!" and making new friendships that way.

— White, bisexual/queer, cisgender woman

Chapter 7

COMING OUT AT WORK

Coming out at work can be a risky business.

On the one hand, LGBTQ activism has clearly demonstrated that claiming social space in the business world can have a significant impact on larger social perceptions of sex and gender minorities. With this increased recognition has come an opportunity to organize for workplace equality, and LGBTQ folks have fought long and hard to gain medical benefits for partners, hospital visitation rights, and access to legal marriage. In some places, LGBTQ people have gained workplace protections against being fired for sexual or gender identity. This kind of recognition depends on being recognizable—coming out.

On the other hand, coming out is literally exposing, and exposure can be dangerous. People who have been publicly identified as polyamorous have lost their jobs, housing, friends, and families of origin, as well as custody of their children. Obviously, not everyone who comes out as polyamorous will experience such devastating consequences, but it is important to remember that polyamory can really freak some people out, and they might react poorly. Coming out at work means risking negative reactions, yet hopefully encountering some positive ones as well.

Before: What to Consider Before Coming Out at Work

Prior to coming out to folks at work, consider several issues carefully.

First, why are you thinking of coming out? If you would like to be closer to coworkers you're friendly with, and you feel emotionally safe with them and would trust them with sensitive information, then hiding what you do on the weekends or changing pronouns/numbers when talking about your life can feel like a terrible chore. An imminent holiday party including significant others can also spur people to consider coming out to coworkers. Establishing a serious and lasting polyamorous relationship can also provide the impetus to come out. Whatever your reason for wanting to come out at work, make sure it is good enough to outweigh the potential risks.

Second, how are your coworkers likely to react? If they are a kind and open-minded bunch and you feel confident they will welcome your polyamorous partners with open arms, then by all means contribute to the group's warm fuzzy vibe by being yourself. If, however, they are prone to vicious gossip, backstabbing, and undermining others, then you might reconsider exposing yourself to their ridicule.

Third, what will happen if you lose your job due to your polyamorous or otherwise nonmonogamous identity? Are you able to support yourself without this job? If you are self-employed, you will probably not fire yourself, but coming out may affect your relationships with your clients or other professional contacts. If you have a lot of personal, professional, and financial freedom, then you are safer to come out. For those in jobs they cannot afford to lose, especially in conservative industries or locales, it might be inadvisable to come out at work.

Fourth, how emotionally close do you want to be to your coworkers? Is it worth the risk to invest in honesty with them?

If you think it is, then consider coming out—at least to the people you trust. Would you prefer to maintain a friendly professional distance from coworkers and keep your social sphere separate? Then you are probably not even considering coming out to coworkers.

Fifth, what are your company's policies and regulations? If they have a workplace nondiscrimination policy, read it to see if sexual and/or gender identities are protected. If policies provide protections for folks in same-sex relationships or trans folks, then they are likely to at least consider including polyamorous relationships in that same umbrella, because some people think polyamory is a form of sexual orientation. If there are no policies, then it is possible that your company has not considered the issue yet, that they are in the process of considering it, or that they have already thought about it but do not want to protect or are not prioritizing protecting sex and gender minorities. As we discussed in chapter 1, some companies include morality clauses in their hiring packets. For employees who have signed a morality clause, being exposed as polyamorous can be no different from being exposed as cheating, because the problem is extramarital sex, not consent among the multiple partners.

Considering (at least) these five issues can help you to decide whether your workplace is safe and how much you are willing to risk to be out.

During: What to Do When Coming Out

Once you have decided to come out, you must decide how to do so. Consider being very selective about whom you tell, especially at first. Test the waters with a trusted friend, and see how it feels to have someone at work know about your relationships. Choose a private time and place to come out, where you will have the opportunity to chat with your coworker and deal with any unexpected reactions. Avoid sensationalizing it or setting it up as a big reveal, and if possible, work it into conversation in a natural way. When the casual approach is not possible, be direct and nondramatic, and make it simple and clear. Provide your coworker with a few educational resources if they ask or seem confused, but avoid the appearance of recruiting or converting them.

After: What to Do After Coming Out

Coming out as polyamorous at work provides you with several opportunities. First, you can openly advocate for workplace equality for polyamorous folks and other sex and gender minorities. If you want more information on how to do so and what kinds of advocacy you might consider, check out the organization Out & Equal (outandequal.org). Similarly, you can form coalitions with other sex and gender minorities, as well as other groups that have not traditionally held power, in order to create a more equitable workplace. Finally, if coming out at work has blown up in your face and things are intolerable there, you can always look for a different job. It is not ideal, but if people at work start treating you poorly, you need to remind yourself that you are not stuck in a terrible environment and that you can go somewhere else.

§

Stories: Coming Out at Work

Kitty Is Out to Only Some People in Her Professional Life
Because I am a small-business owner and my business depends on referrals, I always use a pseudonym when writing about poly-amory. My accountant is a wonderful person and sends me a lot of business, but I have no doubt that if she knew I was polyam-orous those referrals would instantly stop, because she is very

conservative and religious. Anything that could affect my income due to discrimination, I don't tell. So my rule of thumb is that if I am earning money with someone and it's not related to polyamory, then I don't tell them about polyamory. I sang with a band that was very traditional, so I didn't tell them. I used to work for a small advertising agency, and my boss made derogatory remarks about a client, whom he referred to as one of "those dirty filthy swingers." I knew right away that I could never tell him about my lifestyle.

On the other side, I am also an entrepreneur and am out to my entrepreneurial colleagues worldwide. They have all accepted me; no one has ever said anything negative to me about it. I once ran into a woman at a conference, and she mentioned how much she appreciated my taking the time to explain polyamory to her, because she had confused it with orgies and now understood it much better. That was fun, realizing that I could work on educating the world about polyamory, one person at a time.
— White, heterosexual, cisgender woman

Sarah Was Out at Work as Bi, But Not Poly
I taught at Gallaudet University for nine years, between 1997 and 2006. It felt extremely easy to be out as bisexual but very difficult to be out as poly. Being poly was different and was not supported in the same way. I never really came out to my department, even though some other faculty members did know. I never felt like I could bring multiple partners to the departmental picnic or anything like that. It felt so different and so new, and no one else was talking about it. I felt unsafe coming out as poly and thought that my colleagues would be judgmental about it.
— White, Jewish, bisexual, cisgender woman

Chris Gets Written Up
I have experienced indirect discrimination from employers because of my openness about poly.

I used to work for a historically Black college/university in residence life managing a dorm. I would have my partners come in, and dorm residents would meet them. The residents were excited and would ask me, "You can do what?" I would be up until three or four in the morning talking with the residents about relationship best practices and how not to lie to your partners. One time a guy knocked on my door at about three in the morning and told me that he was practicing being open and honest and he was really excited—"She really likes me!"

The staff were older, conservative African Americans, and one of my coworkers pulled me aside once and told me I should be a lot quieter about my relationships. I was quite surprised, because he was gay, and I would have thought he of all people would not be telling me to be more closeted. Didn't he just fight for marriage? If he had also been the subject of inequality and discrimination, why didn't he understand others who were fighting for that same respect? Did he not just fight that discrimination himself? As a mixed-race person in a relational minority group, I kind of expected to find support from my other sex- and gender-minority compatriots. It was an unpleasant surprise that he—a Black gay man—would tell me to hide my identity.

There was also the time I got a write-up for the fact that I was in the dorm with two of my partners. We were kickin' it downstairs, not kissing or anything inappropriate. My boss told me that I should not be out and about with them like that, that it did not look good. I got written up for unprofessional behavior simply because I had two partners with me in my leisure time, which was also where I worked, because I lived in the dorm too. That was several years ago now, but even in my current employment with older, conservative African American people, I have to be careful of what I say, or I will face a glass ceiling. Being in the Poly Leadership Network and keeping my ear to the ground, I hear about a lot of people getting discriminated against at work, in the justice system, and in child custody matters, or being seen as deviant and having Child Protective Services try to

take their kids. There is so much the poly community has to deal with because polyamory is not legally recognized and is seen as a socially deviant concept. I look forward to the day that people of all relationship structures can breathe easy in the United States.
— Black, heterosexual, cisgender man

Lucy Gets Fired for Coming Out

Sometimes it's important to share sad stories. Though it's difficult, we can choose to keep our eyes open to the pain and horror around us, because it is through this pain and horror that we have the opening to grow. The opening for true transformation. Through opening our heart to the feelings of fear and distaste at the way things currently are, we can choose something else. We can use the way things are now as an inspiring springboard for initiating a new way.

In the summer of 2015, my world seemed to explode. I had been employed part-time as a Reiki practitioner and workshop leader with a nonprofit alternative wellness center in a small, socially conservative Midwestern town. Though I'd spent a number of rather challenging years building my reputation as a local teacher and healer, I'd been pleasantly surprised at the overall receptivity of the community to Reiki, an energy-healing modality that directly contradicts the premise that one must seek a doctor (a traditional authority) for healing, and proposes that one can, in fact, learn how to heal oneself. A radical practice indeed! I was loving my work and loving my daily life.

My work with the wellness center had been in the beginning stages, with promises of more work to come once certain grants and other sources of funding could be obtained. A few months after I joined the staff, the director began ignoring my emails. Then, my name disappeared from the organization's website. I sent a query to a colleague. No response. I tried to reach the director again. No response. At that point, I became really busy. I had just published some writings about polyamory and was busy networking and launching a new local support group for poly.

I was so busy, in fact, that when a colleague from the wellness center (also a dear friend) phoned me, I had somewhat forgotten about the puzzling lack of communication—so we spent the first half hour or so exchanging news about our daily lives: her new pet dog, my new potential girlfriend. Finally, I asked about the website. After a shaky pause, she told me she was very sorry, but that our director had been intentionally ignoring me. "Why?" I asked.

"Polyamory," she said. "Your writing, your speaking, your being so open about it all." I then learned that the decision to fire me had actually been made weeks ago. Apparently our director lacked the time and courage to tell me herself, and had requested that my friend deliver the news.

A few days later, I emailed the director. I asked for her honesty; I asked her to explain more of the details and the rationale behind her decision. In her reply, she wrote how she had been "directly approached by two influential people" from our town. These people warned her that association with me might negatively impact future donations. And here she donned the victim role: "I had no choice," she wrote, but to listen to them, because so much of what the nonprofit did was "relying on volunteers and donations." She then explained that their position on polyamory was not her personal position. She told me she had no problem with what I did or how I lived my life. In closing, she wrote, "I think you're a lovely and well-balanced person with much to offer the community."

What the director did not understand was that by taking the action she did, the position of those two influential people *became* her position. The personal is the political, and the political is the personal. There is no dividing line, no neat boundary separating the two. What we do in our private/personal lives is a reflection and demonstration of our political/public lives; what we do in our political/public lives is a reflection and demonstration of our private/personal lives. When police officers arrested Rosa Parks for refusing to move to the back of the bus, were these not the police officers' political *and* personal actions? We could say that the police officers who arrested her that day were victims too—we could say they had no choice but to obey the segregation laws. But is that true? Were they really choiceless victims? Or could the officers have, instead, empathized with Parks, and eschewed the laws of hatred and discrimination in Montgomery?

In a world where money seems to rule all, the pressure to submit to the whims of the rich and powerful was simply too much for my director to bear, despite her liking my work and despite our friendship. The director had a mission. She wanted to bring health care and wellness to those in our community, so the decision was made to fire me, because she didn't want those who were attempting to manipulate her to get in the way of that mission.

There's more to the story. Incredibly, the day after I discovered I'd been fired from the wellness center, I was fired from my other part-time job as well, at a nonprofit community education center. The main reason they offered for the firing was alleged sexual misconduct. The allegations, based solely on rumors and gossip, were being used as a smokescreen. The reality was that they didn't want a person who was vocal about polyamory on their staff. A few weeks later, the director apologized to me, saying that indeed the firing had been due to false rumors, not truth, and that the decision had been made in too much haste. But she did not offer me my job back.

These incidents altered the course of my life forever. I learned firsthand why so many LGBTQ people feel so pressured to stay in the closet in small towns. When I reached out to friends and mentors in the poly movement, such as Elisabeth Sheff and Robyn Trask, the general response was "Lucy, your news is sad, but, unfortunately, it is not shocking." They told me that many, many cases similar to mine have been reported to the National Coalition for Sexual Freedom in recent years. Not only are polyamorous people and others in alternative relationship styles in danger daily of losing their jobs, but they also run the risk of losing their children or even landing in jail as a result of sexual allegations, rumors, and hysteria. Indeed, coming out is not an easy or straightforward issue in our current times.

I still live in this small Midwestern town. I left for a while (in anger and disgust) but then moved back, because my intentional family is here, and because I wanted to continue the healing work that I began here. I continue to facilitate the poly support group and speak at the local university when they invite me. Recently, I received some legal threats from one of the organizations that had fired me, which is why I am publishing this story under a pseudonym.

If you are reading this story and are considering coming out of the closet, please know that I support whatever you choose to do that feels right for you. I cannot tell you what choice is best. However, I can say this: In my time as a healer and a guide, I have learned that sometimes it's best not to try to logically weigh out a problem with pros and cons, but rather to get still inside yourself, and feel into how your heart, body, and intuition are trying to guide you. You know what to do. You are beautiful, and your relationships are beautiful, and the world will feel the impact of your love no matter what you decide.

Thank you for your love.
— White, heteroflexible, cisgender woman

Kevin Doesn't Get Personal

I am out at work, but when I am at work, I don't really talk about my personal life. Because I work contract positions, I could be at work for six months, one year, or two years, so I don't spend a lot of time getting that personal. If someone asks me what my weekend was like, I'll say, "My wife, my girlfriend, and I did this" or "I hung out while my wife and her boyfriend went to some event" or "My wife watched the kids while my girlfriend and I went on a trip." So I'll be honest about it, but those are sorta few and far between.

— Kevin Patterson, a Black, heterosexual, cisgender man and
   founder of *Poly Role Models*

There's Nothing to Be Ashamed Of

I'm lucky in that the majority of the work I've done while having been polyamorous has been in an industry where polyamory is accepted. I also have a "day job" that is a bit less accepting. I was really concerned about coming out at that job, because I needed the job, but I didn't feel comfortable hiding my relationships.

When I started sharing about myself and my life, I made the decision that I would just talk about my partners the way I would talk about my partner were I monogamous. It was a bit nerve-racking, as I didn't want to jeopardize my new job. Luckily my coworkers were super respectful, and if they were curious they asked me very polite questions. I think that were I to hide it from others I would start to feel ashamed of my lifestyle or guilty that I may be hurting my partners. I am not ashamed of myself, my life, who I love, or who I am, and I won't let anyone make me feel that way.

— White, bisexual, cisgender woman

Finding Love at Work

I came out to my coworkers after one year of being polyamorous and six months of working with them.

I was in an open relationship with my husband. I was just beginning to date others, and he was not dating.

I first came into contact with Art when I published a blog article about Findhorn, a new age community in Scotland where we had both spent time. He emailed me to say that he liked the article, and I emailed him back saying that I had been a student on the study abroad program that he directed a number of years ago. We then had a Skype conversation where we chatted about our mutual interests in ecovillages, sustainability, and climate change. At the time, he was starting a social venture related to climate change. I was unemployed, and I decided to volunteer to help him get it started.

Our cohorts in the social venture were two other investors. We all lived in different states, and every week we would meet online for a conference call. As a way for us to connect person-ally, Art would lead a check-in at the beginning of every call for each of us to share what was going on in our lives. My cohorts usually shared the activities of their children and other work they were doing. I did not have children and didn't have much to share, except that I was exploring polyamory and going through a lot of turmoil, both with my husband and internally, but I did not share about that.

Six months later, I had a phone conversation with one of the investors where I shared my interest in polyamory and its rele-vance to sustainability. He was interested and supportive. At the next conference call, I shared this conversation with the group and came out about being polyamorous. Art immediately shared that he had been in an open relationship with his wife for twenty years and that polyamory had brought a great deal of growth and happiness to his life. He was not only okay with my coming out, but also relieved, because he was now also able to share honestly about his life and deepen his relationship with us, which was important to him as well as to our working relationship.

Art and I then began to have conversations about polyamory. He shared with me the history of his relationships, and how he came to embrace polyamory after being initially reluctant when his wife wanted to open their relationship. My husband was also reluctant at that point, and Art talked with the two of us to help us with what we were going through.

After five months of talking, Art and I met in person. We were immediately attracted to each other. Even though we knew an intimate relationship was possible, we still had our work relation-ship to consider, and the distance was an undesirable factor. We still felt that a relationship was worth pursuing and talked to our partners and our cohorts about it. They were a little surprised, and some expressed concern over the impact it would have on our work relationship, but they were all supportive.

At the time of this writing, Art and I have been dating for eight months. Our relationship has been a dazzling journey in

intimacy, compatibility, and creative collaboration. While difficult
to separate the two, my personal relationship to him has slightly
strengthened my commitment to our work relationship. I've also
enjoyed getting to know his partner and learning about all the
relationships in our pillow network. We are currently writing a
blog about polyamory to share our experiences and help others
grow in this lifestyle: consciouspolyamory.org.
— Asian, heterosexual woman

Chapter 8

COMING OUT AT SCHOOL

How and if a polyamorous person or family publicly claims their polyamorous status in school settings depends a lot on the age of the student, as well as how relevant it is and the status of the family. As when coming out to friends, to family, or at work, many people will want to consider the implications carefully prior to making any decisions about coming out at school.

Before: What to Consider Before Coming Out at School

Before you come out at school—whether it's your school or the one your children go to—consider the context carefully.

Elementary School

There is almost no need for children in elementary school to come out to their peers as being from a polyamorous family. Even if their peers noticed "extra" adults around, it is unlikely that they would be able to formulate questions about the adult relationships involved. So many children come from divorced families now that extra adults are completely normal figures in kids' lives. It is far more likely that other parents or teachers will notice the multiple nature of the relationship, so preparing kids to answer their questions is important if other adults will be around enough to appear as family members. Parents can encourage kids to tell others that these folks are friends, and leave it at that. If teachers or other parents continue to ask questions, the child can refer the inquisitive adult to their parents.

Parents face a far more complex job when considering whether to come out at their children's elementary schools. Similar to considering the safety and utility of coming out at work, parents should consider the social environment of the school, the level of conservatism or religiosity, and their reasons for coming out. For parents in accepting schools, whose partners are fully integrated into the children's lives and therefore relevant to their schooling, and/or whose children are likely to include partners in drawings or discussions of family, coming out might be the right choice. For parents who live in religious or conservative school districts, who do not trust their school officials to be reasonable about sexual diversity, and/or whose partners are not relevant or visible to people at school, it might make more sense to remain closeted, or to at least be discreet and provide information on a need-to-know basis.

Middle School/Junior High

While elementary school students are rarely sophisticated enough to develop deep understandings of complex adult relationships, students in middle school or junior high are a whole different story. Awakening to their own sexual selves, these tweens are aware of adult interactions in a new way and more aware of their peers' families as points of comparison. Explaining family variations to these more observant peers can be difficult, but luckily they generally have short attention spans and are easily distracted (at least for the moment). Children uncomfortable with giving extensive explanations can simply tell their friends that the extra adults are their parents' friends, even their "quirky" friends if that would help to explain any unconventional hours or behavior. Changing the subject works well too.

For those kids with close friends who are themselves accepting and open-minded, simply telling the truth can be liberating, or not a big deal at all. If children are not sure how their friends might react, asking a test question before coming out can provide a better sense of what that friend might say. When asked what they think of gay marriage, if a child says that they have a gay aunt they love dearly, then that child might be safe to tell. A child who responds that all gay people are going to hell might not be the right person to tell.

Not much changes for parents between elementary school and junior high when it comes to dealing with school officials or other parents. Remaining on a need-to-know basis tends to work well. When the need to know arises, providing straight-forward information about polyamorous families is probably your best bet. Less can be more, so feel free to be vague and let others ask questions.

High School

By high school, most students are aware of their parents' sex lives to some extent. Usually teens prefer not to think or talk about their parents' sexual relationships and will most likely not bring them up extensively with their peers. Also, not only is meeting peers outside of the home fun for many teens, but it also forestalls questions about family form, because the teens are not around their families at that point. Many teens who do not want to have to explain their dad's boyfriend will meet their friends at the mall, the movies, or the park to avoid deal-ing with the questions entirely.

The same testing technique described above can be useful for high school students deciding whether coming out as a polyamorous family member is safe or wise. Teens are not as easily distracted as tweens and are more likely to return to the question of who exactly these people are. Creating a group of "my parents' weird friends" that are up to arcane adult stuff goes a long way toward casting them all as benignly eccentric and leaves room to respond to other questions with "I don't know; they do their own thing."

Deciding to attempt polyamorous relationships as a teen is becoming increasingly common, and teens who want to come out as polyamorous themselves might find support among their peers in a gay–straight alliance or another club or organization serving LGBTQ students. Refusing to identify with any specific sexual or relationship orientation is common among youth (especially queer youth), so polyamorous teens might not feel the need to make a coming-out announcement to friends and simply be content conducting their lives and relationships without labels.

At this stage, parents may need to field more questions from their children's peers, either about their own polyamorous relationships or about things happening in the teens' lives. Teens' peer groups will view some polyamorous parents as sex-positive role models or resources with advice and information. Respondents from Dr. Elisabeth Sheff's book *The Polyamorists Next Door* reported that their teens' friends would come to them asking for reliable information about sex-related topics like orgasms, birth control, and STIs, as well as with relationship questions, like how to communicate with friends who had been fighting or how to deal with bullying at school. Adults who find themselves in these situations need to consider setting new boundaries or rethinking existing ones. They also need to decide how much direct assistance they feel comfortable providing and how much communication they are willing to have with the parents of their children's friends as a result of their offering information and help.

For some, simply providing teens with a nonjudgmental and supportive environment for self-exploration and expression will change their lives for the better. In other cases, parents must face difficult decisions, such as if a teen wants help getting an abortion or doesn't want to report a date rape to authorities.

Because sex and gender minorities can come under extra scrutiny from authorities if something goes wrong, it behooves polyamorous parents to err on the side of caution when it comes to other people's children. If you have liquor in the house, keep it locked or otherwise inaccessible so teens don't end up intoxicated at your house. Even if your teen does not drink, other curious youth might investigate your liquor stash and abscond with some booze or drink it at your place. Keep sex toys and pornography stored discreetly in adult spaces, and be sure to provide adequate supervision of teen activities at your residence.

College

Coming out as polyamorous in college is generally not a big deal, because college hookup culture already makes nonmonogamy the norm rather than the exception. Being emotionally intimate with multiple partners is what might strike others as unusual, but the presence of multiple romantic or sexual partners or prospects is standard operating procedure for many college students in the United States today. A major exception to this rule is the more conservative sexual environment found in many religious colleges, where students espouse and sometimes practice conservative sex lives based on heterosexuality, chastity before marriage (especially for women), and sexual exclusivity during marriage.

Graduate School

Coming out as polyamorous in graduate school can be no big deal and simply blend in with other graduate student sexual shenanigans, or it can make a lasting impression on your future colleagues and potentially tank your chances for post-graduation employment with those folks. If the rest of the grad students are open about their sex lives, then you might be safe being honest about yours as well. However, if they are judgmental, cutthroat, sex negative, and/or conservative, you might want to omit that part of your life from conversations with them. Because some of the other grad students will continue on to be leaders in their (and your) field, they might later reappear in your life as members of hiring committees, collaborators, competitors, or potential employers. If you are in a conservative field, and competitors knowing that you are polyamorous would give them leverage against you, it might be better to keep that information more private in graduate school. If, however, you are in a field where sex and gender minorities are accepted and valued, then coming out as polyamorous in graduate school can be a good thing, because it will allow you to be authentic with others and form explicit alliances with other sex and gender minorities.

Teachers and Professors

Professionals who work in schools blend issues of coming out at work and coming out at school. Historically, parents and administrators have been reluctant to "allow" known sexual minorities—mostly people in same-sex relationships—to teach young children. This lingering fear is rooted in false assumptions that nonheterosexuals are more likely to be sexual predators or that they will somehow "infect" previously heterosexual youth with same-sex desire. Even though both assumptions have been disproven by research, it does not stop uneducated or bigoted people from patrolling the sexuality of teachers. This same attitude might certainly be extended to firing teachers who are exposed as nonmonogamous.

As students get older, concern about teacher sexuality tends to wane. By the time students are in college, there is far less oversight of extracurricular sexuality, and most of the administrative focus on professorial sexuality is limited to preventing sexual harassment among faculty, staff, and students. If professors are nonmonogamous in their private lives, administrators and parents are less likely to be concerned (unless it is a religious institution; then those institutions may require a morality clause, similar to conservative employers).

Being openly polyamorous, or any kind of sexual or gender minority, as faculty, staff, or administration in colleges or universities is probably safer than in many other settings, because colleges and universities tend to allow for a greater range of thought and questioning, which fosters variation, freedom, and creativity. Outside of religious institutions, colleges are infamous as hotbeds of liberalism, and research shows that prejudice in general and sexual stigma in particular decline as education increases. Essentially, educated people are less likely to be homophobic, blatantly racist, or openly sexist. Education does not make people perfect, and certainly bigotry remains at all levels of society, but people in higher education are more likely to be liberal than in some other fields, and that makes it a bit safer to be out as anything unconventional in academia.

§

Stories: Coming Out at School

Osirus (Twelve Years Old) Comes Out at School

I came out at school recently because once Amanda became more a part of my life, I felt like I should talk about her. Before, when Amanda just came into the relationship, it was less open because she was new. I told my homeroom teacher first. She has a rainbow flag by her desk. Then I told my principal and my student government advisor. All three of them were open and said I could talk to them if I had something to get off my chest. I told them I wanted to organize an event for families who had lost family members in the Orlando nightclub shootings, so I will try to do this now. I am the charity coordinator for the school system.

Some of the kids at school didn't understand, so I tried to explain. Half of the kids thought it was cool and okay. The other half either still didn't understand or thought it was bad because it was against their religion. Of the people who already knew about it, there were people who disagreed and people who were okay. I am kind of seen as the weird kid for having a family like this, but I'm fine with it.

Advice: if people think your family is weird or you are weird, just ignore them. It doesn't matter what your family is. It matters if your family loves you and takes care of you. I don't care who my mom and dad date as long as they're nice and treat my parents well.

Amanda has been to almost everything I've had. She's been to all of my concerts. She's gone to most of my assemblies this year. She came to a lot of my student government stuff and to my speech to become the vice president. There was one thing she couldn't make it to, so she watched the video. My mom's family is supportive, my daddy's family is not okay at all, and Amanda's family is still confused. It matters what happens in the relationship, not outside it.

— White, cisgender boy

Sara's (Osirus's Mom's) Pleasant Surprise
I am fairly shocked that the teachers were as accepting as they were. It may be because Osirus has all As and is an honor roll student. He has excelled in school and skipped a grade. It would be hard for them to say there were problems at home with him having that level of achievement. I think this plays into the acceptance of the teachers. His teachers have been supportive,

and he has been "outgoing" about it. When one of the kids said some things that were upsetting, the guidance counselor called and was supportive. The principal has gotten to know Amanda, and she has been very involved at school. Osirus was taught never to be ashamed of his family or to feel like he had to hide. It didn't come up as much when he was younger, but now that Amanda is more involved and is almost always at the house, it's hard for him to talk about his life without talking about Amanda being involved in it.

I had to sign him up for honors classes, and the administrator was like, "Is it just going to be you, or is it going to be any of the other Osirus adults?" And when I got there it seemed like she was excited to meet the poly people. She was talking about Osirus's grades and all of the things he was doing, like sports and student government and book club. She said it was nice that he had so many people in his life who could help him do all of these things. She asked about division of time and who does what, etc. It seems like the school has really gotten it.

The only thing that I've had trouble dealing with as a parent was him coming home upset because of the nasty things that some of the other kids have said to him. It's really hard to see that, and it really sucks. I wouldn't change the way he's done things, because it was his choice. He did a family tree for Spanish class and put Amanda on the family tree as the lover of his parents. I wouldn't change that he's done those things or that he's proud of his family.

— Sara, a White-dominant-identified, bi/pansexual, cisgender woman

Kevin Is Aggressively Out

My wife and I are aggressively out. If there's someone in our lives, we call them by their names. Whether that's a friend, partner, boyfriend, girlfriend, whatever. When we talk about the people in our lives, the people that we love, we don't present it as if it's something to be ashamed of or something we're scared to talk about. Instead, we just talk about it. And if someone asks us an honest question, we'll give them an honest answer, but that rarely happens. Usually it's just as simple as "Hey teacher, my wife and I are polyamorous, my girlfriend sometimes might pick up the kids from school," and that's the end of the conversation.

— Kevin Patterson, a Black, heterosexual, cisgender man and
founder of *Poly Role Models*

Chapter 9
AFTER COMING OUT: BEING POLYAMOROUS

Once you have come out, or have begun the ongoing process that is coming out, you might begin to wonder exactly what it means to be polyamorous. There is no simple answer to that, and various people in various polyamorous communities do not necessarily agree on a single unified definition of polyamory. Some people see it as a lifestyle based in choice and freedom, while others see it as a form of sacred sexuality, a sexual orientation, or even a social movement. It is all of those things and more. Above all, being polyamorous is what you make it, how you define it, and what kinds of connections and interactions you create. All of that happens in an existing social framework, though, and no one can craft a relationship in a vacuum.

Polyamorous Community

One of the sad realities of polyamorous life is that people sometimes lose friends when they come out. While that can be painful, remember that a friend who rejects you because of how your romantic relationships is a friend you have already lost. If you can't be yourself with your friends, they're not really your friends. It also clears the way to make new friends in polyamorous communities. Socializing with other polyamorists can have many benefits. For one, you don't have to constantly explain your relationships and then worry about what people are going to think of you. If others are exploring the idea of polyamory as well, they probably have at least some degree of openness to it.

Finding Community

While we list many resources to connect with polyamorous community at the end of the book, we wanted to highlight a few of them here as well. Meetup is a website that helps people coordinate meetings with others in their local area who have similar interests, and it can be a great place to look for polyamory-related groups. Another good online source is FetLife. Although it caters primarily to kinky folks, FetLife has a huge range of folks talking about all sorts of things that can be useful for polyamorists as well—especially kinky polyamorists. Loving More is an organization that provides education, conferences, public advocacy, and community connections with many other groups. It also previously published a magazine; past print articles, along with newer online articles, can be found online (lovemore.com/magazine). Facebook, of course, offers many different polyamory groups as well.

Creating Community

Not finding what you want in an existing group? Consider starting one yourself. We have found that it works really well for us to set regular events and invite all the polyamorous people we know. Hosting game nights, going to happy hour, and setting up something public or private that allows you to build a safe space can all help create community. Post your events on Facebook and Meetup, plus any other social networking site you like. When you're creating a community space, be sure to make it an inclusive, safe space for people of all abilities and backgrounds.

Consider using a meeting to make clear guidelines about keeping people safe, beginning with a discussion of what the people in the group consider safe. You can make rules about things like confidentiality and appropriate behavior around touching. One of the challenging jobs for group leaders is helping people feel empowered to ask for what they want while still respecting boundaries. Consent is one of the main things groups generally emphasize at every level, all the way down to asking someone explicitly if they want a hug. If you need ideas about how to talk about consent, consider checking out the National Coalition for Sexual Freedom's Consent Counts project, which offers lots of good advice about establishing consent.

Polyamorous Etiquette

In many cultures, there is an expected yet often unspoken agreement about how the members of a community are supposed to behave. Polyamorous people are already going against the grain of expected community behavior. Because of that, we strongly encourage brushing up on your etiquette for how to behave around other people, both polyamorous and monogamous.

Monogamous Settings

When you go to events outside of the poly community, you'll probably be in a monogamous setting, where bringing more than one date is likely to raise some questions.

Bringing Multiple Partners to a Social Event
In some settings, polyamorous multiples can simply blend in, and other people might assume you're just friends. In other situations, it's going to be apparent that you're more than just friends, in which case you'll have to have a conversation with your partner(s) about how to handle questions when they come in. It can be a good idea to establish a safe word and/ or escape route in case one of the partners feels uncomfortable and would like to leave. Having a poly resource website or book name handy in case someone brings up uncomfortable questions can also be a useful tactic. If you are not out in your community but you want to bring multiple partners to events, consider how your other partner(s) may feel if you are addressing your "approved" partner (such as a spouse or an already-introduced partner) as your only partner.

Bringing Multiple Partners to a School Event
Many schools and teachers already work with blended families that include children from different marriages and multiple parents. Rebecca feels that it is wise to at least let the teacher know that your child has multiple parents. Tamara has found that teachers often do not ask who's who and why they are at school events. Even in situations where it's very apparent that something "unusual" is going on, they don't generally ask a lot of questions. If you need to talk about your relationships for some reason (for instance, if there is bullying or issues with peers at school), then you need to have a conversation about how safe you feel discussing your relationships at school.

Bringing Multiple Partners to a Work Event
Some workplaces are very open socially, and it wouldn't be an issue to show up to the company picnic with multiple partners. Other employers expect that you bring only one partner to events. Talking to your partners before the event about how people are addressed and what information coworkers are

given can help folks prepare for the event and help partners decide whether they wish to attend.

Awkward Confrontations

Preparing a game plan for possible responses if people ask you awkward or uncomfortable questions can help make impending social functions less frightening. Try to remain calm and avoid getting defensive. Because most people simply don't understand polyamory, try to assume good intentions unless something is very clearly meant disrespectfully. Remember that you don't owe anyone an explanation for your lifestyle, nor are you required to be a polyamory ambassador.

Polyamorous Settings

Going to poly events can be liberating, since you don't have to think about how to act with your dates or worry about awkward questions. But, just like in any other community, it's important to be aware of certain cultural norms.

Introducing Partners

Finding out from your partner in advance how they want to be identified at an event can go a long way toward avoiding mistakes. It can also help to clarify how they want you to talk about them in your daily life.

Asking Others Out

It can be tempting to try to show respect for someone's existing relationships by asking them out via their partner rather than asking the person directly. This is a mistake, however, because it can give the (hopefully erroneous) impression that you think their partner has control over them. This can be especially problematic if you are asking a man for permission to ask a woman out, because it gives the very patriarchal impression that you need to go through him to access "his" woman. Instead, go to the person you are interested in and ask directly. If they have a requirement that they need to have a conversation with their partner(s), then it is up to them to manage that boundary.

Touching

The polyamorous community can be super affectionate, but you *must* ask before touching someone. Ask "Do you hug?" or even ask with body language. Open your arms and wait for the person to come toward you. Listen to body language. A hug lasts only until the first person lets go.

Preferred Pronouns

In some ways, polyamorous communities are on the social fringes. This can make them into queer-friendly environments that allow and even celebrate gender diversity. But because you cannot always tell someone's gender simply by looking at them, it is important to ask people about their preferred gender pronouns (she/her, he/him, they/them, etc.). Avoid making assumptions about people's social identities and genitalia—even if you think their gender is obvious. Once someone tells you which pronouns to use, respect that choice. It can be awkward to use the plural "they" instead of the singular "she/he," but once you practice it gets easier. If you slip up, apologize and give yourself a break. If you do it continuously, then it may come across as a microaggression in which you intentionally misgender someone, so try to be aware of respecting people's self-definitions.

Respect the Space

This can mean anything from knowing and following the rules set by the people who are hosting an event to offering to help in the kitchen instead of expecting to be served.

Cultivating Compersion

Take every opportunity to practice *compersion*, or joy at your partners' relationships with others. That openness is probably what attracted you to them in the first place. Use and strengthen your empathy skills by helping others, practicing active listening, cultivating curiosity, and reading books that help you see things in new ways and from different perspectives.

Polyamorous Drama in Polyamorous Spaces

When you are in a polyamorous space, there will be an understanding that this sort of thing is hard, and your emotions may be triggered. People are likely to pick up on any negative emotions that you might be displaying. Expect that people will ask about what you're going through and offer to help. Do take advantage of the knowledge and support of the community to help you develop better emotional regulation skills for your jealousy and other issues.

Be Nice

Also phrased as "Don't be a dick" in polyamorous circles, take some time to think about things from others' perspectives as if they were happening to you. Cultivate compassion.

If You Mess Up

Because polyamory is a relatively new relationship style without a lot of role models for appropriate behavior, it is unsurprising that people sometimes make mistakes. If you accidentally breach polyamorous etiquette, own up and apologize. Just because you didn't intend to hurt someone or behave poorly doesn't mean you didn't. Talk to the person you offended, ask what you can do to make up for it, and find out what you can do different next time. It is okay to respectfully ask how you messed up—but be sure to truly listen to the response instead of planning how you will rebut what the person is saying.

Beware of Common Mistakes

The more people and personalities you have in one space, the more likely that mistakes are going to be made in interpersonal relationships and at community events. Making a mistake can be embarrassing, but it's important to sit with that discomfort to understand how you can do better in the future. Learning from your mistakes and growing through them allows you, your relationships, and the polyamorous community to thrive.

Here are some of the mistakes we've seen people make when joining the polyamory community:

- Using discussion groups as dating pools. Instead, if you meet someone you're interested in, get to know them better outside of the group before asking them out.
- Assuming that because a person is open to multiple relationships or sex with others it automatically means they will have a relationship or sex with you. Instead, assume that people have boundaries, and find out what they are.
- Talking endlessly about the hot bi babe you're looking for to complete your relationship. Instead, get to know people by asking them questions about themselves, and by being open about who you are and why people might want to get to know you.
- Assuming some relationships are less valuable than others—the "everyone is in a hierarchy" headspace. Instead, ask people how they structure their relationships.
- Questioning others' sexual orientations. Instead, assume that each person is the expert on themselves and believe what they tell you about their personal identities.
- Expecting that all the members of your new polycule will adjust their other relationships to make room for you. Instead, find out how they have accommodated new people before, and ask for your needs to be met in a way that blends with the existing relationships.

- Assuming that you're always going to agree with all polyamorous folks. Instead, remember that polyamorous people are as diverse as any other community.
- Looking down on anyone for having issues that you've outgrown or don't experience. Instead of assuming you are more evolved than the other person, be aware that people encounter all sorts of situations and issues in life and have varying skill sets and resources with which to deal with them.
- Outing without permission. Instead, ask people whom they are out to and whom they are comfortable being out to. When in doubt, keep quiet.

The Polyamorous Agenda

While several activist organizations work for a polyamorous political agenda, the mainstream polyamorous community seems fairly apolitical. Not only is the polyamorous community newer and smaller than the gay and lesbian movement upon which polyamorists have patterned themselves (unconsciously, to large degree), but polyamorous communities are too diverse and dispersed to create even a single definition of polyamory, much less a unified political agenda. Plus, polyamorous folks can get so many of their practical relationship needs met with access to existing social arrangements (such as being able to legally marry as a couple even if they have other partners) that they have less impetus to seek social change.

Even so, there are a few organizations and groups that do attempt to find a common thread in a polyamorous political agenda. Most of them focus on civil and human rights, custody of children, and protection from discrimination. For instance, Loving More is a nonprofit dedicated to advancing public education about polyamory and providing advocacy for polyamorous folks. Its mission is "to educate people about and support polyamory as a valid choice in loving relationships and family lifestyle." It organizes conferences and serves as a community organizing hub, and has helped raise funds for the first big custody case involving a child of a polyamorous parent. It continually interacts with press outlets to educate the general public about polyamory.

The Canadian Polyamory Advocacy Association is possibly the most politically oriented polyamory organization. It "promotes legal, social, government, and institutional acceptance and support of polyamory, and advances the interests of the Canadian polyamorous community generally" by organizing and posting legal documents relevant to polyamory, explaining how the "poly majority" differs from the patriarchal minority, and tracking the impact of court decisions about multiple-partner marriage in Canada.

One of the reasons we chose to close with the idea of poly activism was to complete the circle of what we brought up in the introduction: the political utility of being out as a polyamorous person. The success of gays and lesbians in gaining political traction has been directly linked to their willingness to take the risks associated with coming out. The same could work for polyamorous folks. If you have the social privileges and safety to come out, please do! If not, then work for equality and social justice for polyamory and all people, however you can, and come out when/if it works for you. Either way, we wish you the best in your journey!

Chapter 10

MOVING FORWARD IN POLYAMORY

When you begin to identify as polyamorous, it may shake you to your core. It may change the way you see yourself, or how you reconcile your personal identity with your personal beliefs. Throughout this book, we have tried to give you the resources you need to navigate this intensely personal journey. In this chapter, we want to give you the support you need. It can be hard, when coming out as polyamorous, to feel supported or encouraged. We've discussed ways in which coming out is a potentially negative experience. You have seen stories of poly-amorous individuals and families, and the ways they managed their coming out.

There is a chance that you will encounter resistance during your coming-out process. You may feel like you are not getting encouragement from anyone around you. You may feel like you do not have support or understanding, but don't be discouraged. There is nothing wrong with you, or with polyamory. You are who you are, and you love who you love.

Your coming-out journey is personal, and it does not need to be defended. If you are worried about coming out because you don't have a support system, it is okay not to. If you feel like you don't have the resources to defend your life, your relationships, or your love, it's okay to take your time to learn from others' mistakes. It is okay to build an educational arsenal full of personal anecdotes and citations from podcasts, books, and blogs so you can give sources to back up your experiences. If you feel like you don't have the support and encouragement needed to come out of the closet, it is completely acceptable for you to take time to become stronger in that closet and build your support structure until you're ready. Take the time to establish your relationships and gain experience. Take the time to find or create a supportive community, whether online or in person, full of people who will love, respect, and support you.

Before coming out, take time to recognize that not everyone will agree with you, respect you, or support you. Not everyone will agree with the way that you do polyamory. It's important to remember that the good often outweighs the bad and that there's no one way to come out to the people in your life. The benefit of polyamory is that you can choose to structure your relationships to fit your needs. The most important relationship you build is with yourself. You become your own support structure, you build your own community, you are responsible for your interactions within your relationships. Recognize your needs, your wants, and your expectations. Recognize your own inner strength, and come out as a proud, happy, and educated polyamorous person!

Glossary

chosen family People who are very important in your life and whom you rely upon, interact with, and think of as family members. Not linked through biology or legal status, chosen family relies upon people's desire to be with each other.

compersion The feeling of happiness or joy associated with your partner's loving someone else. Though sometimes called the opposite of jealousy, it can actually coexist with jealousy, and is another way to react to your partner becoming close to someone else.

consensual nonmonogamy The practice of having more than one relationship at the same time, with the full knowledge and consent of all partners involved.

hierarchical A system of polyamory where one relationship is privileged over others.

metamour Your partner's partner.

moresome Five or more people who are in a relationship together.

nesting partner A partner with whom you cohabitate and share household resources and responsibilities.

new relationship energy The surge of excitement when a relationship first starts and everything is shiny and new.

nonmonogamy The practice of having more than one loving, romantic, and/or sexual relationship.

OPP/OVP Most commonly the one-penis policy, rarely the one-vagina policy, a configuration in which one person can date many people of the opposite sex, but their partners can only date many of the same sex.

polyamory The practice, state, or ability of having more than one loving, romantic, and/or sexual relationship at the same time, with the full knowledge or consent of all partners involved.

polycule A network of people in relationships with each other.

polynate The idea of being out as polyamorous and encouraging other people to also be out as polyamorous.

quad Four people who are all in a relationship with each other.

relationship anarchy A relationship style where relationships are not titled, but are allowed to flow freely and change at will.

solo polyamorist A person who is interested in multiple partners but does not want to have a primary or nesting partner.

triad Three people who are all in a relationship with each other.

unicorn A single bisexual person who is open to dating a couple.

V A configuration where one person is involved with two people who are not involved with each other.

Z Two Vs that are attached.

Resources

Books

- *Designer Relationships: A Guide to Happy Monogamy, Positive Polyamory, and Optimistic Open Relationships* by Mark A. Michaels and Patricia Johnson
- *The Ethical Slut: A Practical Guide to Polyamory, Open Relationships & Other Adventures* by Dossie Easton and Janet W. Hardy
- *More Than Two: A Practical Guide to Ethical Polyamory* by Franklin Veaux and Eve Rickert
- *Opening Up: A Guide to Creating and Sustaining Open Relationships* by Tristan Taormino
- *The Polyamorists Next Door: Inside Multiple-Partner Relationships and Families* by Dr. Elisabeth Sheff
- *Stories From the Polycule: Real Life in Polyamorous Families* by Dr. Elisabeth Sheff
- *When Someone You Love Is Polyamorous: Understanding Poly People and Relationships* by Dr. Elisabeth Sheff

Organizations

- Canadian Polyamory Advocacy Association, polyadvocacy.ca
- Loving More, lovemore.com
- Out & Equal, outandequal.org
- World Polyamory Association, worldpolyamoryassociation.net

Podcasts

- *Life on the Swingset—The Swinging & Polyamory Podcast*, lifeontheswingset.com/category/podcast/

- *Loving without Boundaries: Lessons in Practicing Polyamory*, lovingwithoutboundaries.com/podcast/
- *Multiamory*, multiamory.com/podcast-summary/
- *Polyamory Weekly*, polyweekly.com
- *Poly in the Cities*, polyinthecities.com
- *Sex Out Loud*, tristantaormino.com/sex-out-loud/about/

Professional Lists

- Kink Aware Professionals Directory, https://ncsfreedom.org/key-programs/kink-aware-professionals-59776
- Open List, http://openingup.net/open-list/
- Poly-Friendly Professionals Directory, polyfriendly.org

Blogs

- *Conscious Polyamory: A Blog about Loving More than One*, consciouspolyamory.org
- *Dirty Stories—John Stark*, wesleeptogether.blogspot.com
- *Elisabeth Sheff*, elisabethsheff.com
- *Graydancer*, graydancer.com/blog
- *The Inn Between*, theinbetween.net
- *Jenny on the Page*, jennyonthepage.blogspot.com
- *Kimchi Cuddles*, kimchicuddles.com
- *Loving without Boundaries*, lovingwithoutboundaries.com/blog
- *Mistress Matisse*, mistressmatisse.blogspot.com
- *More Than Two*, morethantwo.com/blog
- *The Open Photo Project*, theopenphotoproject.com
- *The Ordinary Extraordinary*, theordinaryextraordinary.com
- *Polyamory in the News*, polyinthemedia.blogspot.com
- *The Polyamorous Misanthrope*, polyamorousmisanthrope.com
- *Poly in Pictures*, polyinpictures.com
- *Poly Role Models*, polyrolemodels.tumblr.com
- *Practical Polyamory*, practicalpolyamory.com
- *Sexis Magazine*, edenfantasys.com/sexis

- *SoloPoly*, solopoly.net
- *Tiny Nibbles*, tinynibbles.com
- *The Twisted Monk*, twistedmonk.blogspot.com

Websites and Discussion Lists

- FetLife, fetlife.com
- LiveJournal Polyamory Community, polyamory.livejournal.com
- Meetup, meetup.com
- More Than Two, morethantwo.com
- Poly Adventures, polyadventures.com
- PolyFamilies, polyfamilies.com
- Poly Living, polyliving.net
- PolyMatchMaker, polymatchmaker.com
- PolyResearchers, groups.yahoo.com/neo/ groups/PolyResearchers/info
- Polyamory Weekly, polyweekly.com

Notes

CHAPTER 1

6 Definition of polyamory
PolyFamilies. (n.d.). Polyamory 101. http://www.polyfamilies.com/
   poly101.html

6 *Green Egg* article
Morning Glory Zell-Ravenheart. (n.d.). A bouquet of lovers:
   Strategies for responsible open relationships. http://caw.org/
   content/?q=bouquet

6 Designer relationships
Mark A. Michaels & Patricia Johnson. (2015). *Designer relationships:
   A guide to happy monogamy, positive polyamory, and optimistic
   open relationships*. San Francisco: Cleis Press.

7 Relationship anarchy descriptions
Autumn. (2013, December 23). Relationship anarchy is not
   polyamory [Blog post]. http://archive.is/FJJQa
Marie S. Crosswell. (2014, March 22). Relationship anarchy basics
   [Blog post]. http://goodmenproject.com/gender-sexuality/
   relationship-anarchy-basics-jvinc/

7 Relationship anarchy quote
Elisabeth Sheff & Megan M. Tesene. (2015). Consensual nonmonogamies in industrialized nations. In John DeLamater &
   Rebecca F. Plante (Eds.), *Handbook of the sociology of sexualities*
   (223–241). New York: Springer.

7 Monogamish
Dan Savage. (2011). Monogamish [Blog post]. http://www.
   thestranger.com/seattle/SavageLove?oid=9125045

9 Research on polyamorous families
Elisabeth Sheff. (2014). *The polyamorists next door: Inside multiple partner relationships and families.* Lanham, MD: Rowman and Littlefield.

11 Solo polyamory quote
Aggie Sez. (2014, December 5). What is solo polyamory? My take [Blog post]. http://solopoly.net/2014/12/05/what-is-solo-polyamory-my-take/

12 Anchor partner quote
Cunning Minx. (2010, November 15). A replacement for "primary/secondary" [Blog post]. http://polyweekly. com/2010/11/a-replacement-for-primarysecondary/

12 Nonmonogamy in mainstream gay male culture
Paul Andrews. (2014.) How gay men make decisions about the place of extra-relational sex in their committed relationships. *Psychotherapy in Australia, 20*(3), 40.

12 Influence of religion in African American communities
Human Rights Campaign. (n.d.). Religion and coming out issues for African Americans. http://www.hrc.org/resources/religion-and-coming-out-issues-for-african-americans

12 Fear of judgment in Black polyamorous people
Elisabeth Sheff & Corie J. Hammers. (2011). The privilege of perversities: Race, class, and education among polyamorists and kinksters. *Psychology & Sexuality, 2*(3), 198–223.

14 Polyamory in the 1800s
Loraine Hutchins. (2001). Erotic rites: A cultural analysis of contemporary United States sacred sexuality traditions and trends [Doctoral dissertation]. http://www.lorainehutchins.com/writing/

14 Brook Farm quote

Loraine Hutchins. (2001). Erotic rites: A cultural analysis of
contemporary United States sacred sexuality traditions and trends
[Doctoral dissertation]. http://www.lorainehutchins.com/writing/

14 Oneida Community quote

Raymond Lee Muncy. (1973). *Sex and marriage in utopian
communities: Nineteenth-century America.* Bloomington, IN:
Indiana University Press.

14 Nashoba quote

Loraine Hutchins. (2001). Erotic rites: A cultural analysis of
contemporary United States sacred sexuality traditions and trends
[Doctoral dissertation]. http://www.lorainehutchins.com/writing/

14 "Libertines"

Robert M. Ireland. (1989). The libertine must die: Sexual dishonor
and the unwritten law in the nineteenth-century United States.
Journal of Social History, 23(1), 27–44.

14 Sexual freedom in men versus women

Mary Ann Glendon. (1989). *The transformation of family law: State,
law, and family in the United States and Western Europe.* Chicago:
University of Chicago Press.

14 "Lawful adultery"

Stephen Collins. (1997). "A kind of lawful adultery": English attitudes
to the remarriage of widows. In Glennys Howarth & Peter C.
Jupp, (Eds.), *The changing face of death: Historical accounts of
death and disposal* (34–47). London: Palgrave Macmillan UK.

15 New ideas about marriage

Stephanie Coontz. (2006). *Marriage, a history: How love conquered
marriage.* New York: Penguin Group.

15 Sandstone

Loraine Hutchins. (2001). Erotic rites: A cultural analysis of contemporary United States sacred sexuality traditions and trends [Doctoral dissertation]. http://www.lorainehutchins.com/writing/

15 Kerista quote

Maura I. Strassberg. (2003). The challenge of post-modern polygamy: Considering polyamory. *Capital University Law Review, 31*, 439–563.

16 Forming connections online

John A. Bargh & Katelyn Y.A. McKenna. (2004). The Internet and social life. *Annual Review of Psychology, 55*, 573–590.

17 Infidelity rates

Adrian J. Blow & Kelley Hartnett. (2005). Infidelity in committed relationships II: A substantive review. *Journal of Marital and Family Therapy, 31*(2), 217–233.

17 Sexual activities in young adults

Martin A. Monto & Anna G. Carey. (2014). A new standard of sexual behavior? Are claims associated with the "hookup culture" supported by general social survey data? *Journal of Sex Research, 51*(6), 605–615.

18 Social constructs of infidelity

Naomi P. Moller & Andreas Vossler. (2015). Defining infidelity in research and couple counseling: A qualitative study. *Journal of Sex & Marital Therapy, 41*(5), 487–497.

18 Josh Duggar on client list for cheating website Ashley Madison

Dana Ford. (2015, August 21). Josh Duggar after Ashley Madison hack: "I have been the biggest hypocrite ever." *CNN*. http://www.cnn.com/2015/08/20/us/josh-duggar-ashley-madison/

18 Infidelity linked to age, religious behavior, and educational level

David C. Atkins, Donald H. Baucom, & Neil S. Jacobson. (2001). Understanding infidelity: Correlates in a national random sample. *Journal of Family Psychology, 15*(4), 735–749.

18 Internet expands opportunity for cheating

Russell B. Clayton, Alexander Nagurney, & Jessica R. Smith. (2013). Cheating, breakup, and divorce: Is Facebook use to blame? *Cyberpsychology, Behavior, and Social Networking, 16*(10), 717–720.

Russell B. Clayton. (2014). The third wheel: The impact of Twitter use on relationship infidelity and divorce. *Cyberpsychology, Behavior, and Social Networking, 17*(7), 425–430.

CHAPTER 2

25 STI transmission in consensually nonmonogomous relationships

Justin J. Lehmiller. (2015). A comparison of sexual health history and practices among monogamous and consensually nonmonogamous sexual partners. *The Journal of Sexual Medicine, 12*(10), 2022–2028.

25 Communication within polyamorous communities

Justin J. Lehmiller. (2015). A comparison of sexual health history and practices among monogamous and consensually nonmonogamous sexual partners. *The Journal of Sexual Medicine, 12*(10), 2022–2028.

26 Custody challenges

Elisabeth Sheff. (2014). *The polyamorists next door: Inside multiple partner relationships and families.* Lanham, MD: Rowman and Littlefield.

27 Acceptance of family members

Joyce Baptist & Katherine R. Allen. (2008). A family's coming out process: Systemic change and multiple realities. *Contemporary Family Therapy, 30*(2), 92–110.

Lisa K. Waldner & Brian Magruder. (1999). Coming out to parents: Perceptions of family relations, perceived resources, and identity expression as predictors of identity disclosure for gay and lesbian adolescents. *Journal of Homosexuality, 37*(2), 83–100.

29 STI risk assessment

Justin J. Lehmiller. (2015). A comparison of sexual health history and practices among monogamous and consensually nonmonogamous sexual partners. *The Journal of Sexual Medicine, 12*(10), 2022–2028.

39 Polyamorous possibility

Elisabeth Sheff. (2013, November 4). Fear of the polyamorous possibility. *Psychology Today.* https://www.psychologytoday. com/blog/the-polyamorists-next-door/201311/ fear-the-polyamorous-possibility-5

CHAPTER 4

64 Same-sex polyamorous families

Elisabeth Sheff. (2011). Polyamorous families, same-sex marriage, and the slippery slope. *Journal of Contemporary Ethnography, 40*(5), 487–520.

67 Finding a lawyer

The Kink Aware Professionals Directory. https://ncsfreedom.org/ key-programs/kink-aware-professionals-59776

73 Older people in polyamorous relationships

James R. Fleckenstein & Derrell W. Cox II. (2015). The association of an open relationship orientation with health and happiness in a sample of older US adults. *Sexual and Relationship Therapy, 30*(1), 94–116.

73 Positive environments for children

Elisabeth Sheff. (2014). *The polyamorists next door: Inside multiple partner relationships and families*. Lanham, MD: Rowman and Littlefield.

CHAPTER 7

133 Polyamory as a form of sexual orientation

Elisabeth Sheff. (2016). *When someone you love is polyamorous: Understanding polyamorous people and relationships*. Portland, OR: Thorntree Press.

Ann E. Tweedy. (2011). Polyamory as a sexual orientation. *University of Cincinnati Law Review, 79*(4), 1461–1515.

CHAPTER 8

148 *The Polyamorists Next Door*

Elisabeth Sheff. (2014). *The polyamorists next door: Inside multiple partner relationships and families*. Lanham, MD: Rowman and Littlefield.

CHAPTER 9

161 Empathy skills

Elizabeth Seward. (n.d.). 5 ways to cultivate empathy for others. http://www.happify.com/hd/5-ways-to-cultivate-more-empathy/

163 Loving More mission statement

Loving More. (n.d.). About Loving More. http://www.lovemore.com/aboutus/

164 Canadian Polyamory Advocacy Association mission

Canadian Polyamory Advocacy Association. (n.d.). About. http://polyadvocacy.ca/about/

Index

Also From Thornapple Press

Polysecure: Attachment, Trauma and Consensual Nonmonogamy

Jessica Fern

"Polysecure is smart, readable, pathsetting, and deeply caring. And practical. Jessica Fern presents abundant material that will inform poly-friendly therapists everywhere, and she offers six particular strategies that will help polyfolks and their beloveds to become more 'polysecure' in their relationships."

— Lindsay Hayes, *Polyamory in the News*

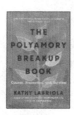

The Polyamory Breakup Book: Causes, Prevention, and Survival

Kathy Labriola, with a foreword by Dossie Easton

"Mandatory reading for those considering an adventure into the world of consensual non-monogamy."

— Ken Haslam, MD, founder of the Ken Haslam Polyamory Archives, the Kinsey Institute, Indiana University

Nonmonogamy and Neurodiversity

Alyssa Gonzalez

The third title in the More Than Two Essentials series, this practical guide explores how nonmonogamous relationships do not belong exclusively to the neurotypicals, but to us all.

Ask Me About Polyamory:
The Best of Kimchi Cuddles

Tikva Wolf

With a foreword by Sophie Labelle

"The warm and open style, and great way of getting complex things across simply, makes it one of the best relationship comics out there."

— Dr. Meg-John Barker, author of *Rewriting the Rules*

More Than Two: A practical guide to ethical polyamory

Franklin Veaux and Eve Rickert

"More Than Two may well be the best book on polyamory I've ever read. No joke, it's really that fantastic."

— Andrea Zanin, *Sex Geek*

Playing Fair: A Guide to Non-Monogamy for Men Into Women

Pepper Mint

"Playing Fair is a brilliant road map for a more conscientious approach to ethical nonmonogamy."

— Kevin Patterson, founder of the *Poly Role Models* blog

About the Authors

Tamara Pincus is a licensed clinical social worker and AASECT-certified sex therapist who runs a private practice in the Washington, DC, area. She specializes in working with kinky, polyamorous, and LGBTQ clients, and she has been active in alternative sexuality communities since 1998. She has spoken around the country on issues related to ethics in sex therapy, consent culture, polyamory, and BDSM. She has published articles and pamphlets including *What Professionals Need to Know about BDSM* and *What Is Polyamory and Why Do Social Workers Need to Know About It?*

Rebecca Szymborski (formerly Hiles) is a dating, relationships, and sexual wellness coach. She has contributed to Sexpert.com and xoJane.com, and has had her writing featured on *Everyday Feminism*. She was voted one of the Top 100 Sex Blogging Superheroes of 2014 and 2015.

About the Authors